EVERYONE**CAN**COOK
for celebrations

ERIC AKIS

EVERYONE**CAN**COOK
for celebrations

seasonal recipes for festive occasions

whitecap

Whitecap Books is known for its expertise in the cookbook market and has produced some of the most innovative and familiar titles found in kitchens across North America. Visit our website at www.whitecap.ca.

Edited by Elaine Jones
Proofread by Amelia Gilliland
Cover and interior design by Jacqui Thomas
Typesetting by Setareh Ashrafologhalai
Food photography by Michael Tourigny except Roasted Tomato Tart (page 117) by Gary Hynes
Food and prop styling by Eric Akis
Author photo by Cheryl Warwick

Printed in China

LIBRARY AND ARCHIVES CANADA CATALOGUING IN PUBLICATION

Akis, Eric, 1961–
    Everyone can cook for celebrations : seasonal recipes for festive occasions / Eric Akis.

ISBN 978-1-55285-993-3

    1. Cookery. 2. Menus. 3. Entertaining. I. Title.

TX731.A34 2009   642'.4   C2009-902677-5

The publisher acknowledges the financial support of the Government of Canada through the Book Publishing Industry Development Program (BPIDP) and the Province of British Columbia through the Book Publishing Tax Credit.

09 10 11 12 13   5 4 3 2 1

CONTENTS

EVERYONE**CAN**COOK
for celebrations

This book is dedicated to everyone who understands the importance of taking the time to sit down with family and friends, enjoy a fine meal and celebrate life.

ACKNOWLEDGMENTS

With this being the fifth volume in my Everyone Can Cook series, I now realize, more than ever, that I could not create such well-received books without the help of a very talented group of people.

Thanks to the team at Whitecap Books for being so dedicated to publishing the best cookbooks around. In particular, I want to thank publisher Robert McCullough for believing in me, a small-market author with big dreams. To editor Taryn Boyd, thanks for being so darn organized, flexible and so inspiringly positive during the months-long process of creating this book.

Thank you to Whitecap's Michelle Mayne, Setareh Ashrafologhalai, Amelia Gilliland, Lesley Cameron and Grace Yaginuma for your talented efforts in making this book look and read so well. I must also give applause to freelance editor Elaine Jones, who skillfully did the first edit of this book.

People often buy cookbooks because they contain beautiful food photos and in this case I must once again pass on my accolades to photographer Michael Tourigny (michaeltourigny.com), who took the mouth-watering images in this book. To Michael's assistants Laura (Beetroot) Scotten and Marilize Botha, thanks for your help in producing those images and for appearing in those that required some action. You're the best!

To my friend and fellow chef Laura Agnew, thank you for helping to prepare the mountain of food required for the photos.

Lastly, and most importantly, thank you to my darling wife, Cheryl, and my fine and caring son, Tyler, for being so supportive during those early mornings, weekends and other times at home my mind was focused on creating this book, not on you. You've both given me so many reasons to celebrate—I am truly blessed.

INTRODUCTION

Everyone loves a celebration, and food is often central to its enjoyment, whether it's a long weekend barbecue with friends, a family feast at Thanksgiving or a romantic dinner for two to ring in the New Year.

The last thing you want to feel during the lead-up to these occasions is stress. For those in charge of creating the menu and preparing the dishes that will be served, that can indeed occur, even among accomplished home cooks.

All sorts of questions that cause culinary unease can arise when planning for your special occasion, such as what kind of food to serve, the quantities needed and how to get it all done and still find time to celebrate and visit with everyone else sitting around the table.

If these and other issues get your blood pressure rising before hosting a gathering, *Everyone Can Cook for Celebrations: Seasonal Recipes for Festive Occasions* is a book designed for you. It will help you to relax, enjoy the preparation process and drink in the accolades you'll receive by creating a celebratory meal your guests will rave about.

Everyone Can Cook for Celebrations offers a wide range of inviting recipes laid out in chapters that generally follow the seasons, such as "Celebrate Spring!," "Summer Long Weekends" and "December Gatherings." At the end of each chapter you'll find menus for a variety of celebrations, such as an anniversary dinner, an Easter brunch, a Father's Day feast and an elegant New Year's Day dinner. The introduction to each menu may include touches that will make the occasion even more special, suggestions for simple side dishes to serve with the dishes listed and advance preparation tips.

One of the best parts about the easy-to-follow, delicious recipes in this book is that most of them can be partially or entirely readied in advance, sometimes even a day or two ahead, and this information is provided in the recipes. This removes the pressure of trying to whip up a range of dishes all at the last minute and frees up more time for you to do what you are supposed to do at a party—celebrate!

At some celebrations you'll have a table full of guests and at others, such as a romantic Valentine's Day dinner, it will be just two of you sitting at the table. That is reflected in the recipes in the book: you'll find many that will feed a crowd and others designed for smaller, more intimate get-togethers.

Throughout the book, informative sidebars offer tips on some of the tasks you'll need to undertake before and during a celebratory meal, such as properly chilling and opening sparkling wine, determining when a turkey is cooked and deciding how much cheese to buy for that fine cheese board you want to serve.

As in the first four books in my bestselling Everyone Can Cook series, the recipes are designed for all levels of cooks. The dishes focus on using accessible ingredients readily found in most supermarkets. "Eric's options" included with each recipe offer suggestions for substituting some ingredients or adding others to bring the dish to another level.

With *Everyone Can Cook for Celebrations* in your cookbook library, you'll never again find yourself stuck in the kitchen instead of sharing a festive time with your guests. It will become your seasonal, go-to guide when hosting a special occasion, whether it's on a cold winter morning, a balmy summer evening or a golden autumn day.

WINTER PARTIES

CHAPTER ONE

LEEK and POTATO SOUP with a DRIZZLE of CREAM

preparation time · 20 minutes
cooking time · about 20 minutes
makes · 4 servings

These two winter vegetables—leeks, with their mild onion/garlic flavor, and potatoes, which love to soak up other tastes—blend beautifully in this classic soup. A drizzle of cream just before serving adds a last-second touch of richness.

ERIC'S OPTIONS
For a tangy, rich taste, top each bowl of soup with a little crumbled blue cheese.

2 Tbsp	olive oil	30 mL
2	medium leeks, white and pale green part only, halved lengthwise, washed, and sliced	2
1	garlic clove, chopped	1
3 Tbsp	flour	45 mL
4 cups	chicken or vegetable stock	1 L
1	medium baking potato, peeled and cubed	1
½ tsp	dried tarragon	2 mL
to taste	salt and ground white pepper	to taste
4 tsp	whipping cream	20 mL
1 Tbsp	chopped fresh parsley	15 mL

Heat the oil in a pot over medium heat. Add the leeks and cook until softened, about 3 to 4 minutes. Add the garlic and cook 1 minute more. Mix in the flour until well combined, and cook, stirring, 1 to 2 minutes more. While stirring steadily, slowly pour in the stock. Mix in the potatoes and tarragon. Bring the soup to a simmer and cook until potatoes are very tender, about 15 minutes.

Purée the soup in a food processor or blender, or in the pot with an immersion blender. Bring back to a simmer; season with salt and pepper. Ladle the soup into heated bowls. Use a 1 tsp (5 mL) measure to drizzle the cream in a spiral on top of each serving. Sprinkle with parsley and serve.

CRUNCHY CRUDITÉS with LEMON BASIL MAYONNAISE

preparation time · 25 minutes
cooking time · none
makes · 8 servings

Crisp raw vegetables and a tangy dip provide a nice, light appetizer to serve before the main course.

ERIC'S OPTIONS
Instead of lemon basil mayonnaise, serve the crudités with roasted garlic Caesar dressing (page 125) for dipping.

1 cup	mayonnaise	250 mL
¼ cup	chopped fresh basil	60 mL
1 tsp	finely grated lemon zest	5 mL
2 Tbsp	fresh lemon juice	30 mL
to taste	freshly ground white pepper	to taste
12	radishes, trimmed	12
12–16	snow or snap peas	12–16
12	small cauliflower florets	12
12	small broccoli florets	12
½	large yellow bell pepper, cut into small wedges	½
½	large orange or red bell pepper, cut into small wedges	½
½	medium English cucumber, cut into sticks	½
2	medium carrots, cut into sticks	2

Combine the mayonnaise, basil, lemon zest, lemon juice, salt and pepper in a small mixing bowl. Spoon the mayonnaise into a serving bowl and place in the middle of a decorative platter. Artfully arrange the vegetables around the mayonnaise. Cover and store the crudités in the refrigerator until ready to serve. Can be prepared a few hours in advance.

SWEET and SOUR COLESLAW with CRANBERRIES and PECANS

preparation time ·	20 minutes	
cooking time ·	none	
makes ·	8 servings	

There's a rainbow of color in this vegetable-rich, sweet and tangy coleslaw accented with dried fruit and nuts.

ERIC'S OPTIONS
Instead of cranberries, use raisins in the coleslaw. Substitute unsalted roasted cashews for the pecans.

Amount	Ingredient	Metric
¼ cup	cider vinegar	60 mL
3 Tbsp	vegetable oil	45 mL
1 Tbsp	granulated sugar, or to taste	15 mL
1 tsp	Dijon mustard	5 mL
to taste	salt and freshly ground black pepper	to taste
4 cups	thinly shredded green cabbage (about ½ small head)	1 L
1	small carrot, grated	1
1	small yellow bell pepper, cut into small cubes	1
2	green onions, thinly sliced	2
½ cup	dried cranberries	125 mL
½ cup	pecan pieces	125 mL

Place the vinegar, oil, sugar, mustard, salt and black pepper in a large bowl and whisk to combine. Add the remaining ingredients, toss to coat the vegetables and serve.

PULLED TURKEY SANDWICHES

preparation time	·	30 minutes
cooking time	·	about 1 hour 55 minutes
makes	·	8 sandwiches

This is an oven-cooked version of a southern pulled meat sandwich using turkey instead of the frequently used pork.

ERIC'S OPTIONS
Bone-in turkey thigh and breast are sold at most supermarkets. If you prefer all dark meat, then use 2 turkey thighs in this recipe. If you prefer white meat, use 2 turkey breasts in this recipe.

Serve these sandwiches with sliced dill pickles and raw or sautéed onions.

2 lb	bone-in turkey thigh, skin removed	1 kg
2 lb	bone-in turkey breast, skin removed	1 kg
2 tsp	chili powder	10 mL
1 tsp	ground cumin	5 mL
½ tsp	paprika	2 mL
½ tsp	salt	2 mL
½ tsp	coarsely ground black pepper	2 mL
1¼ cups	barbecue sauce	310 mL
¾ cup	beer	175 mL
¼ cup	honey	60 mL
¼ cup	apple cider vinegar	60 mL
8	hamburger buns, warmed	8

Preheat the oven to 450°F (230°C). Line a baking sheet with parchment paper; place the turkey pieces on the baking sheet. Combine the chili powder, cumin, paprika, salt and pepper in a small bowl. Rub the mixture all over the turkey. Roast the turkey 30 minutes, or until dark and richly colored on the exterior. Remove the turkey from the oven. Lower the oven temperature to 325°F (160°C).

Combine the barbecue sauce, beer, honey and vinegar in a wide, ovenproof pot or Dutch oven. Bring to a simmer over medium-high heat, then add the turkey. Cover and cook in the oven for 75 to 80 minutes, or until the turkey is falling-apart tender. Remove the turkey from the sauce and set in a bowl. When cool enough to handle, pull the turkey into shreds and discard the bones. Skim any fat from the sauce and bring the sauce to a simmer over medium heat. Add the turkey shreds to the pot and toss to coat with sauce. Sandwich the hot turkey in the buns and serve.

GRILLED CORNED BEEF and IRISH CHEDDAR SANDWICHES

preparation time · 10 minutes
cooking time · 16–18 minutes
makes · 4 sandwiches

I like to serve this hearty, Irish-inspired meat and cheese filled sandwich with a glass of Guinness.

ERIC'S OPTIONS
Instead of corned beef, make these sandwiches with thinly sliced roast beef or pastrami. Instead of rye bread, make these sandwiches with sourdough bread.

5 Tbsp	butter, softened	75 mL
2	medium onions, thinly sliced	2
8	slices rye bread	8
4 tsp	Dijon or other hot mustard, or to taste	20 mL
4 Tbsp	mayonnaise, or to taste	60 mL
½ lb	thinly sliced corned beef	250 g
6 oz	Irish cheddar cheese, thinly sliced	175 g

Melt 2 Tbsp (30 mL) of the butter in a skillet over medium-low heat. Add the onion and cook, stirring, about 10 minutes, until golden and sticky; remove from the heat and set aside. Butter 4 slices of the bread on 1 side. Set buttered side down on a work surface. Spread the unbuttered sides with the mustard and mayonnaise. Place an equal amount of corned beef on each of the 4 bread slices. Top with the onions and sliced cheese. Spread one side of the remaining 4 bread slices with butter and set on the meat-, onion- and cheese-topped bread slices, buttered side up. Heat 2 large, nonstick skillets over medium-low to medium heat. When hot, set 2 sandwiches in each skillet and cook for 3 to 4 minutes per side, until golden brown and the cheese is melted. Cut each sandwich in half and serve.

ABOUT CORNED BEEF

The word "corned" in corned beef was derived from 17th century English use of the word *corns* to refer to small grains, such as the coarse salt used to cure meat. Beef brisket is the cut of choice for corned beef. It's a tough, thick cut taken from the breast section of the animal. It has a nice amount of fat, and that, along with brining and long, slow cooking, results in an end product that is succulent, tender and beautifully flavored. Corned beef is sometimes also made with other cuts of beef, such as round.

Ingredients in the brine for corned beef can include water, salt, garlic and pickling spices, such as bay leaves, peppercorns and cloves. Once the meat has been brined, it needs to be cooked, and home cooks have a choice on who does that.

Every supermarket and delicatessen sells cold, cooked corned beef, which they will slice as needed for you. They also sell pieces of corned beef packed in brine, which can be cooked at home, usually by slowly simmering the meat until very tender.

SPAGHETTI and MEATBALLS for TWO FAMILIES

preparation time	·	20 minutes
cooking time	·	about 45 minutes
makes	·	8 servings

This tasty recipe serves eight. If you're a family of four, why not invite another family of four over for an Italian-style dinner party? The kids can help set the table (perhaps with a red and white checkered table cloth and matching napkins) and choose the Italian music—can you say Dean Martin?

ERIC'S OPTIONS
Give the meatballs a more complex, richer taste by making them with an equal mix of ground beef, pork and veal.

2½ lb	lean ground beef	1.25 kg
2	large eggs	2
½ cup	breadcrumbs	125 mL
¼ cup	milk	60 mL
2–3	garlic cloves, chopped	2–3
1 tsp	dried oregano	5 mL
1 tsp	dried basil	5 mL
1½ tsp	salt	7 mL
1 tsp	freshly ground black pepper	5 mL
6 cups	marinara sauce (see Note)	1.5 L
1 cup	water	250 mL
2 lb	spaghetti	1 kg
for tossing	butter or olive oil (optional)	for tossing
for grating	chunk of Parmesan cheese	for grating

Preheat the oven to 350°F (180°C). Line a large baking sheet with parchment paper. Place the beef, eggs, breadcrumbs, milk, garlic, oregano, basil, salt and pepper in a large bowl and mix until just combined. Moisten your hands with cold water. Roll the meat into 1½-inch (4 cm) balls and set on the baking sheet. Roast the meatballs for 25 minutes, or until cooked through.

While the meatballs cook, place the marinara sauce and water in a large pot over medium to medium-high heat, and bring to a simmer. When the meatballs are cooked, drain well. Add them to the sauce and simmer, partially covered, for 15 to 20 minutes.

While the meatballs simmer, bring a large pot of lightly salted water to a boil. Boil the spaghetti until just tender, about 8 to 10 minutes. Drain well and place in a serving bowl. If desired, to prevent the spaghetti from sticking together, toss with a little butter or olive oil.

Spoon the meatballs and sauce into another serving bowl or serve directly from the pot. Serve with the cheese and provide a grater for diners to top their spaghetti and meatballs with cheese, as desired.

NOTE
Marinara sauce is a herb- and garlic-flavored tomato-based sauce sold in jars or cans at most supermarkets.

BRAISED LAMB SHANKS with HOT MUSTARD, ROSEMARY and WHISKY

preparation time	·	20 minutes
cooking time	·	2 hours 40 minutes
makes	·	6 servings

Rich-tasting lamb made even more rich-tasting by slow-cooking it in a full-flavored mix of ingredients, including spicy mustard and smoky-tasting whisky.

ERIC'S OPTIONS
Instead of lamb shanks, use 6 meaty veal shanks in this recipe. The method and cooking time remain the same.

3 Tbsp	vegetable oil	45 mL
6	lamb shanks, each about 10 oz (300 g)	6
to taste	salt and freshly ground black pepper	to taste
1	medium onion, halved and thinly sliced	1
2–3	garlic cloves, chopped	2–3
1	28 oz (796 mL) can diced tomatoes	1
1 cup	beef stock mixed with 2 Tbsp (30 mL) flour	250 mL
½ cup	Scotch whisky	125 mL
3 Tbsp	tomato paste	45 mL
3 Tbsp	brown sugar	45 mL
3 Tbsp	hot English-style mustard	45 mL
1 Tbsp	chopped fresh rosemary	15 mL

Preheat the oven to 325°F (160°C). Heat the oil in a large skillet over medium-high heat. Season the lamb with salt and pepper. Deeply brown the lamb on all sides and place in a single layer in a large casserole dish. Combine the remaining ingredients in a bowl. Pour over the lamb. Cover and braise the lamb in the oven for 2½ hours, or until the meat is very tender. Skim any fat from the surface of the lamb. Serve the lamb with the sauce on individual plates.

Pictured with Mashed Rutabagas with Buttermilk and Parsley, page 12

MASHED RUTABAGAS with BUTTERMILK and PARSLEY

preparation time · 10 minutes
cooking time · 15 minutes
makes · 6 servings

Mashed rutabagas, called "bashed neeps" in Scotland, are a traditional Scottish side dish with haggis. They also make a nice bed for something meaty and saucy, such as Braised Lamb Shanks with Hot Mustard, Rosemary and Whisky (page 10).

ERIC'S OPTIONS
Try mixing 2 to 3 thinly sliced green onions into the mashed rutabagas.

2½ lb	rutabaga, peeled and cubed	1.25 kg
3 Tbsp	butter	45 mL
½ cup	buttermilk	125 mL
2 Tbsp	chopped fresh parsley	30 mL
to taste	salt and freshly ground black pepper	to taste

Place the rutabaga in a pot, cover with a generous amount of water and boil until very tender, about 15 minutes. Drain well, and then thoroughly mash. Mix in the butter, buttermilk, parsley, salt and pepper.

ABOUT RUTABAGAS AND TURNIPS

Rutabagas are often mistaken for turnips, but the two vegetables, both members of the *Brassica* family, which includes cabbage and broccoli, are quite different.

The skin of the turnip is smoother, thinner and white, and its top is tinged with purple. Turnips are usually smaller than rutabagas and the white flesh is crisper and blander, a result of being harvested when young. Older turnips can become woody and develop a very strong taste.

Rutabagas have long been popular in northern climates. They are hardy and some cold weather before picking can help sweeten the flesh. The flesh of rutabagas is golden and denser than turnip, which makes them good for mashing. The thick skin is golden on the bottom and tinged reddish-brown at the top.

CHILI CUMIN–ROASTED SWEET POTATO WEDGES

preparation time:	·	10 minutes
cooking time	·	30 minutes
makes	·	6 servings

Earthy, sweet wedges of this root vegetable are spicily seasoned, roasted and drizzled with tangy lime juice.

ERIC'S OPTIONS
Instead of light-fleshed sweet potatoes, make the wedges with the orange-fleshed variety, called yams in North America.

3	medium sweet potatoes, washed well and patted dry (see Note)	3
3 Tbsp	olive oil	45 mL
2–3 tsp	chili powder	10–15 mL
2 tsp	ground cumin	10 mL
½ tsp	cayenne pepper	2 mL
to taste	salt	to taste
2 Tbsp	fresh lime juice	30 mL

Preheat the oven to 425°F (220°C). Cut the sweet potatoes in half lengthwise. Cut each half into 4 to 5 lengthwise wedges and place in a large bowl. Add the oil, chili powder, cumin, cayenne and salt and toss to coat the sweet potatoes. Place the sweet potatoes in a single layer on a large nonstick baking sheet. Roast 20 minutes; turn each wedge over and roast 10 minutes more, or until tender on the inside and beautifully browned on the outside. Arrange on a serving platter, drizzle with the lime juice and serve.

NOTE
To get even-sized wedges, choose sweet potatoes of a similar size and shape. The ones I used were about 7 inches (18 cm) in length and 3 inches (8 cm) in diameter.

CHOCOLATE GUINNESS CAKE

preparation time	·	20 minutes
cooking time	·	70–75 minutes
makes	·	12 servings

Guinness, the famous Irish beer, adds a rich color to this moist and chocolaty cake.

1 cup	butter, cubed	250 mL
1 cup	Guinness beer	250 mL
⅔ cup	cocoa powder	150 mL
2 cups	all-purpose flour	500 mL
2 cups	granulated sugar	500 mL
1¼ tsp	baking soda	6 mL
1 tsp	salt	5 mL
2	large eggs	2
½ cup	sour cream	125 mL
for dusting	cocoa powder or icing sugar	for dusting
	vanilla ice cream or whipped cream	

Place the butter, Guinness and ⅔ cup (150 mL) cocoa powder in a medium pot over medium heat. Cook just until the butter melts, whisking to combine it with the Guinness and cocoa. Remove from the heat. Cool the mixture to room temperature.

Preheat the oven to 350°F (180°C). Lightly grease a 10-inch (3 L) springform cake pan. Cut a circle of parchment paper to fit the bottom of the pan and place in the pan. Whisk the flour, granulated sugar, baking soda and salt in a bowl until combined. Add the beer mixture and beat thoroughly. Add the eggs and sour cream and beat until well combined. Spoon and spread the batter into the prepared pan. Bake 70 to 75 minutes, or until the cake springs back when gently touched in the centre. Cool the cake on a baking rack to room temperature.

Unmold the cake and place on a cake plate. Dust the top lightly with cocoa or icing sugar. Serve wedges of cake with a scoop of vanilla ice cream or a dollop of whipped cream.

SCOTCH WHISKY LOAF with CURRANTS and SPICE

preparation time	·	30 minutes, plus time to soak currants
cooking time	·	75–80 minutes
makes	·	1 large loaf

Slices of this loaf taste even better with a little butter on them. The currants soak in whisky overnight, so be sure to factor that in when planning to make this loaf.

ERIC'S OPTIONS
This is a very large loaf, but it can be cut in half, and one half wrapped well and frozen for another time. If your loaf pan is prone to sticking, line it with parchment paper before spooning in the batter.

½ cup	currants	125 mL
½ cup	Scotch whisky	125 mL
2 cups	all-purpose flour	500 mL
½ tsp	salt	2 mL
1 tsp	baking powder	5 mL
½ tsp	ground cinnamon	2 mL
¼ tsp	ground cloves	1 mL
1 cup	butter, softened	250 mL
1⅓ cups	extra fine (berry) sugar (see Note page 74)	325 mL
4	large eggs, separated	4
¼ cup	Scotch whisky	60 mL
⅔ cup	icing sugar	150 mL

Place the currants and the ½ cup (125 mL) whisky in a small bowl. Cover and let the currants soak overnight.

Preheat the oven to 350°F (180°C). Lightly grease a 9- x 5-inch (2 L) nonstick loaf pan with vegetable oil spray. Place the flour, salt, baking powder, cinnamon and cloves in a bowl and whisk to combine. In another bowl, beat the butter and extra fine sugar together until well combined. Add the egg yolks and beat until light and creamy. Add the flour mixture alternately with the currant/whisky mixture until just incorporated.

In a third bowl, beat the egg whites until stiff peaks form; fold them into the batter. Spoon the batter into your prepared pan. Bake in the middle of the oven for 75 to 80 minutes, or until a cake tester inserted in the center of the loaf pulls out clean. Set the loaf, still in the pan, on a baking rack.

Combine the ¼ cup (60 mL) whisky and icing sugar in a bowl. Brush one-third of this mixture over the hot loaf. When it has soaked in, brush the loaf with one-third more of the mixture. Repeat 1 more time. When the last of the whisky mixture has been absorbed, unmold the loaf, cool to room temperature and wrap tightly until you're ready to slice and serve it.

IRISH
COFFEE

preparation time · a few minutes
cooking time · none
makes · 1 serving

Before sharing this recipe, an Irish friend in the restaurant business rhymed off a poem by Joe Sheridan, the barman who invented the drink, that highlights what the flavors in a good Irish coffee should be like: "Cream as rich as an Irish brogue; coffee as strong as a friendly hand; sugar as sweet as the tongue of a rogue; and whisky as smooth as the wit of the land."

ERIC'S OPTIONS
To cheat and make it easier to make the cream sit on top of the coffee, you can lightly whip it to thicken it before spooning it on.

1½ oz	Irish whiskey	45 mL
1–2 tsp	brown sugar, or 1–2 golden sugar cubes	5–10 mL
¾ cup	hot, strong coffee	175 mL
1–2 Tbsp	whipping cream	15–30 mL

Pour the whiskey into a heated glass and add the sugar. Pour in the coffee and stir to dissolve the sugar. Carefully pour the cream against the back of the spoon to help it spread across the surface of the coffee and not sink to the bottom. Serve immediately.

HOT APPLE
COBBLER

preparation time · 30 minutes
cooking time · about 45 minutes
makes · 8 servings

Nicely spiced apples are baked on a sweet, biscuitlike batter that puffs up deliciously around the fruit. It's a wonderful hot dessert to serve on a cold winter night topped with whipped cream or maple walnut ice cream.

ERIC'S OPTIONS
For apple blackberry cobbler, replace 2 cups (500 mL) of the sliced apples with 2 cups (500 mL) of whole fresh or frozen (do not thaw) blackberries.

4 cups	peeled, cored and sliced apples (about 4–5 medium apples)	1 L
½ cup	packed golden brown sugar	125 mL
½ cup	apple juice	125 mL
1 Tbsp	fresh lemon juice	15 mL
1 Tbsp	cornstarch	15 mL
½ tsp	ground cinnamon	2 mL
¼ tsp	ground nutmeg	60 mL
1 cup	all-purpose flour	250 mL
⅓ cup	granulated sugar	75 mL
2 tsp	baking powder	10 mL
¼ tsp	salt	60 mL
1 cup	milk	250 mL
2 Tbsp	butter	30 mL

Preheat the oven to 350°F (180°C). Combine the apples, brown sugar, apple juice, lemon juice, cornstarch, cinnamon and nutmeg in a bowl. In another bowl, whisk together the flour, granulated sugar, baking powder and salt. Stir in the milk until just combined. Place the butter in a 10-inch (25 cm) cast iron, or similar-sized ovenproof skillet, over medium heat. When the butter is melted, remove from the heat and pour the batter into the skillet. Spoon the apple mixture over the batter. Bake for 40 to 45 minutes, or until the batter has risen and puffed around the outer edges and in the center of the cobbler.

MENUS

ST. PATRICK'S DAY LUNCH

Everyone wants to be Irish for at least one day in the year and that is St. Patrick's Day. This lunch that serves 4 will allow you to celebrate in grand style. The soup can be made a day ahead and refrigerated; reheat and drizzle with the cream just before serving. The sandwiches can be assembled in the morning, wrapped and refrigerated, then grilled when you're ready to serve. The cake can be made a day or two in advance, wrapped tightly and stored at room temperature. It serves 12, but you won't mind having leftovers or freezing it for a treat at a later time.

- Leek and Potato Soup with a Drizzle of Cream (page 2)
- Grilled Corned Beef and Irish Cheddar Sandwiches (page 6)
- Chocolate Guinness Cake (page 14)
- Irish Coffee (page 19)

ROBBIE BURNS DINNER

Here's a comforting winter meal for 6 to celebrate Scotland's favorite son and poet, Robbie Burns. Serve the lamb on a bed of the mashed rutabagas. For added color on the plate, add a steamed green vegetable, such as snap peas, rapini or green beans. The loaf can be made a few days in advance of the meal. Keep it tightly wrapped. Like fruitcake, it will improve with age as the whisky, fruit and spices permeate the loaf. A few wee drams of Scotch whisky would accompany this meal nicely and may also cause you to recite a Robbie Burns poem or two.

- Braised Lamb Shanks with Hot Mustard, Rosemary and Whisky (page 10)
- Mashed Rutabagas with Buttermilk and Parsley (page 12)
- Scotch Whisky Loaf with Currants and Spice (page 16)

Continued on the next page . . .

FAMILY WINTER WEEKEND CELEBRATION DINNER

After enjoying a winter activity, whether skiing, skating or building the world's largest snowman, keep the fun rolling by sharing this flavorful and sustaining dinner for 8—a perfect size for feeding a couple of families. The meatballs and sauce can be made the day before and refrigerated until you're ready to reheat them. Get the kids to arrange the crudités on a platter and mix up the simple dip. A few hands could get involved in peeling the apples for the cobbler, which can be baked while you enjoy the meatballs. For an extra-hungry crowd, serve the meatballs with garlic bread.

- Crunchy Crudités with Lemon Basil Mayonnaise (page 3)
- Spaghetti and Meatballs for Two Families (page 8)
- Hot Apple Cobbler (page 20)

FOOTBALL FEAST

Here's a diner-style meal 6 friends can enjoy at home while watching a football championship game or other sporting event. The turkey can be cooked ahead, shredded and refrigerated in its sauce up to a day in advance and reheated when needed. Both the coleslaw and its dressing can be prepared separately several hours in advance and refrigerated until it's time to toss them together and serve. Serve with either ice-cold beer or your favorite soda.

- Pulled Turkey Sandwiches (page 5)
- Sweet and Sour Coleslaw with Cranberries and Pecans (page 4)
- Chili Cumin–Roasted Sweet Potato Wedges (page 13)

RECIPES FOR ROMANCE

CHAPTER TWO

BEAUTIFUL BRUNCH
for TWO

preparation time ·	20 minutes
cooking time ·	10 minutes to warm the croissants
makes ·	2 servings

Here's a simple yet elegant and colorful way to assemble a special brunch for two.

ERIC'S OPTIONS
Instead of brie, serve the grapes and strawberries with a bowl of yogurt. Replace the croissants with warm muffins, made at home or bought from a good bakery.

2–4	croissants	2–4
4	slices of fresh papaya or cantaloupe	4
2	paper-thin slices prosciutto, each cut in half lengthwise	2
¼ lb	wedge brie cheese	125 g
8	fresh strawberries	8
small bunch	seedless grapes	small bunch
2 glasses	freshly squeezed orange juice	2 glasses
1½ cups	sparkling wine (optional)	375 mL
small bowl	raspberry jam or other preserve	small bowl
	cream and sugar	
	coffee or tea	

Preheat the oven to 200°F (95°C). Place the croissants on a baking sheet and warm in the oven 10 minutes. Meanwhile, line a large serving tray with a napkin. Wrap each slice of papaya or cantaloupe with a half-slice of prosciutto and arrange on one side of a decorative plate. Place the cheese, strawberries and grapes on the other side of the plate. Place on the tray, along with the orange juice, sparkling wine, jam, cream and sugar. Add the warmed croissants in a napkin-lined basket or plate to the tray, and finish up with 2 coffee cups and a small spoon and knife. Serve the tray of goodies in a comfortable location, such as the bedroom, in front of the fire or on a sunny patio. Pour the tea or coffee. Sip some orange juice and then top up each glass, if desired, with sparkling wine.

PORTOBELLO MUSHROOM and CAMEMBERT MELTS

preparation time · 20 minutes
cooking time · 10 minutes
makes · 2 servings

A far cry from your basic open-faced broiled cheese sandwich, this decadent snack is made from thin slices of baguette topped with meaty portobello mushrooms and creamy Camembert.

ERIC'S OPTIONS

If you like blue cheese, but still want the creamy texture of Camembert, top each baguette slice with a thin slice of Cambozola. This is a German cheese that has the blue veining found in Italian Gorgonzola cheese and the creamy texture and white-bloom exterior French Camembert is known for.

1 Tbsp	butter	15 mL
1	4- to 5-inch-wide (10–12 cm) portobello mushroom, stem removed and discarded and cap cut into small cubes	1
¼ tsp	minced garlic	1 mL
¼ tsp	finely chopped fresh rosemary	1 mL
2 Tbsp	white wine	30 mL
to taste	salt and freshly ground black pepper	to taste
6	thin slices of baguette	6
3 oz	wedge of Camembert cheese	90 g
6	small rosemary sprigs, for garnish	6

Melt the butter in a small skillet over medium heat. Add the cubed mushroom, garlic and rosemary to the pan and cook 3 to 4 minutes, or until the mushrooms are tender. Add the wine and salt and pepper cook until it has reduced by half; remove the skillet from the heat.

Preheat the oven to 400°F (200°C). Place the baguette slices on a parchment paper–lined baking sheet. Cut the cheese into 6 thin slices just large enough to fit the top of each baguette slice. Top the cheese with the mushroom mixture. Bake for 5 minutes, or until the cheese just begins to melt. Cool slightly, arrange on a plate and garnish each melt with a rosemary sprig before serving.

ABOUT PORTOBELLO MUSHROOMS

It's hard to believe there was a time no one wanted to buy portobellos and growers would, literally, throw them away. That changed in the 1980s, when American marketers looking to improve the image of this mushroom gave it a new name.

The portobello mushroom is simply a fully mature brown mushroom, also called cremini (or crimini), which is a variety of the common white mushroom. As it matures, the mushroom grows quite large, the cap flattens and the gills become fully exposed. Normally one would avoid a brown mushroom that did not have a tightly closed cap, but the more exotic name persuaded people to try it because they believed it was something special, which it turned out to be.

When fully grown, these mushrooms develop a splendid, earthy, almost meaty taste and a dense texture. Portobello mushrooms can be used in all sorts of ways—sliced and fried as a side dish for steak, cubed and added to a stir-fry or grilled whole and stuffed in a burger bun in place of a meat patty. When buying portobellos, choose firm, well-shaped mushrooms free of bruising. You can store them for a few days in the refrigerator in the bag you bought them in, but for the freshest taste, use them as soon as possible.

PLANNING A ROMANTIC DINNER AT HOME

It's fun to eat in restaurants, but some of the most memorable meals a couple can have are in the comfort of their own dining room. There are no disruptions from a waiter or a noisy table next to you, you can set your own pace and you can create an enchanting atmosphere.

Set the stage
To set the stage, use your best dishes, light some candles, dim the lights and match the music and drink to the style of food you are serving, whether it's French, Italian or Japanese.

Be prepared
To ensure things go smoothly, prepare dishes that match your skill level. If you've never made lobster soufflé before, making it the night of a romantic dinner might be a flop in more ways than one. The recipes in this chapter—and in this book—are designed for all levels of cooks. Many can be prepared partially or entirely in advance, which will keep you in the dining room, not in the kitchen, for most of the meal.

Serve bubbly
Champagne has been called "the drink of love" and it, or good sparkling wine, is a great drink to serve with a romantic dinner. It symbolizes lavishness and seems to have been created solely for the purpose of celebration, and its bubbles pair with just about any kind of food, from appetizers to dessert to cheese. See How To Serve Sparkling Wine (page 249).

HEART-SHAPED SMOKED SALMON CANAPÉS

preparation time ·	15 minutes	
cooking time ·	none	
makes ·	2 servings	

Smoky, silky salmon with tangy cream cheese on rye bread is cut into heart-shaped canapés using a cookie cutter sold at kitchenware stores. This is a splendid way to start off a romantic Valentine's Day dinner for two.

ERIC'S OPTIONS
Instead of using pumpernickel, make these canapés on thin slices of sourdough bread.

3 Tbsp	cream cheese, softened	45 mL
1 tsp	chopped fresh dill	5 mL
½ tsp	horseradish	2 mL
to taste	salt, white pepper and fresh lemon juice	to taste
4	thin slices German-style dark pumpernickel bread (see Note)	4
¼ lb	thinly sliced smoked salmon	125 g
2 Tbsp	finely chopped red onion	30 mL
4	dill sprigs for garnish	4

Place the cream cheese, chopped dill, horseradish, salt, pepper and lemon juice in a small bowl and mix to combine. Spread an equal amount of the mixture on one side of each bread slice. Top each bread slice with smoked salmon. Use a heart-shaped cookie cutter, about 3 inches (8 cm) wide, to cut each canapé into a heart. (Wrap and refrigerate the trim left over from cutting the hearts to nibble on for breakfast or lunch the next day.) Set the canapés on a small, attractive plate. Top each with red onion and a sprig of dill, and serve.

NOTE
German-style dark pumpernickel bread is sold at delicatessens and the deli sections of most supermarkets.

ROASTED RED PEPPER SOUP with HEART-SHAPED PARMESAN CROUTONS

preparation time · 25 minutes
cooking time · about 25 minutes
makes · 2 servings

Start a romantic dinner with this Italian-style, Valentine-red colored soup topped with crispy, heart-shaped croutons baked with freshly grated Parmesan cheese.

ERIC'S OPTIONS

Add a little spice to the soup by sprinkling in a few crushed chili flakes when sautéing the onions and garlic. For a richer version, swirl a little whipping cream into the soup just before serving.

CROUTONS

2	slices white bread	2
1 Tbsp	olive oil	15 mL
1–2 Tbsp	freshly grated Parmesan cheese	15–30 mL

SOUP

2 Tbsp	olive oil	30 mL
½	medium onion, sliced	½
1	garlic clove, chopped	1
2 Tbsp	all-purpose flour	30 mL
2½ cups	chicken or vegetable stock	625 mL
2	medium, roasted red bell peppers, coarsely chopped (see Note)	2
1	small baking potato, peeled and sliced	1
½ tsp	dried basil	2 mL
to taste	salt and freshly ground pepper	to taste

To make the croutons, preheat the oven to 350°F (180°C). Use a small, about 1½-inch wide (4 cm) heart-shaped cookie cutter (available at kitchenware stores) to cut each bread slice into 3 to 4 small hearts. Place the hearts on a nonstick or parchment paper–lined baking sheet. Brush the tops lightly with the olive oil. Sprinkle the bread with the cheese. Bake until lightly toasted, about 8 to 10 minutes. Remove from the oven and set aside until the soup is ready.

Continued on page 32 . . .

For the soup, place the oil in a medium-sized pot over medium heat. Add the onion and garlic and cook until softened, about 3 to 4 minutes. Stir in the flour until well combined. Cook, stirring, 1 to 2 minutes more. Slowly, stirring steadily, pour in the stock. Add the roasted peppers, potato and basil, bring to a simmer, and simmer until the potatoes are tender, about 10 minutes.

Purée the soup in a food processor or blender, or in the pot with an immersion blender. Return the soup to a simmer; season with salt and pepper. Add a little extra stock to the soup if you find it too thick. Pour the soup into bowls. Garnish the top of each bowl with croutons and serve.

NOTE

Roasted red peppers are sold in jars or tubs at most supermarkets and Mediterranean-style delicatessens. If you would like to roast your own, see Eric's Options for Roasted Red Pepper Hummus (page 84).

ROMAINE HEARTS with ROQUEFORT CHEESE and CANDIED WALNUTS

preparation time · 20 minutes
cooking time · 10 minutes
makes · 2 servings

Romaine hearts are the center leaves of the romaine, sold in bags at most supermarkets. They make a pleasingly crisp base for this rich salad.

ERIC'S OPTIONS
Instead of roquefort, top the salad with another type of tangy blue cheese, such as Stilton or Danablu.

¼ cup	walnut pieces	60 mL
1 tsp	liquid honey, warmed	5 mL
1½ tsp	red wine vinegar	7 mL
½ tsp	Dijon mustard	2 mL
to taste	salt and freshly ground black pepper	to taste
1 tsp	chopped fresh parsley	5 mL
1½ Tbsp	olive oil	22.5 mL
1	romaine heart, washed, dried and chopped	1
2 oz	roquefort cheese	60 g

Preheat the oven to 300°F (150°C). Line a small baking dish with parchment paper. Place the walnuts in a small bowl, add the honey and stir to coat. Spread the walnuts in the baking dish. Bake 10 minutes, or until the nuts are lightly toasted. Cool to room temperature. Use your fingers to separate any walnuts that are stuck together.

Place the vinegar, mustard, salt, pepper and parsley in a salad bowl and whisk to combine. Slowly whisk in the olive oil. Add the romaine and toss to coat. Divide the lettuce between 2 plates. Top each salad with the walnuts and small nuggets of the cheese before serving.

THE LEGEND OF ROQUEFORT CHEESE

Roquefort is one of the world's most famous cheeses and has an interesting story. According to legend, on a hot day about two thousand years ago, a young shepherd was having his lunch, which included fresh ewe's milk cheese, when he was distracted by a girl he saw in the distance. He put his lunch in a cave near the French village of Roquefort-sur-Soulzon to keep cool, but he did not return for some time. When he finally did, the cheese had a mold on it, but he ate it anyway and liked its taste, and thus was a legendary cheese born.

The mold, called *Penicillium roqueforti*, came from the soil inside the cave and others like it nearby. French law says that only cheese aged in natural caves near Roquefort-sur-Soulzon can be called roquefort. The exterior of the cheese has no rind and is edible and slightly salty. The green-tinged veins of mold running through the cheese are pleasingly tangy. Roquefort can be enjoyed on its own, with fruit and with bread or crackers. Unwrap the cheese and allow it to come to room temperature before serving. The cheese is also used in a wide variety of ways, such as in salads, egg dishes and sauces.

MIXED SALAD GREENS with GOAT CHEESE, ORANGES and ALMONDS

preparation time	·	5 minutes
cooking time	·	5 minutes
makes	·	2 servings

This light and refreshing salad will cleanse and enliven your palate before the main course.

ERIC'S OPTIONS
Instead of almonds, top each salad with 6 pecan halves, lightly toasted a minute or 2 in a nonstick skillet set over medium heat.

2 Tbsp	olive oil	30 mL
2 Tbsp	orange juice	30 mL
1 tsp	Dijon mustard	5 mL
to taste	salt and freshly ground black pepper	to taste
4 cups	mixed baby salad greens	1 L
1	medium orange, peel and pith removed, halved and sliced	1
2 oz	soft goat cheese	60 g
2 Tbsp	sliced almonds, lightly toasted (see Note)	30 mL

Whisk the oil, orange juice, mustard, salt and pepper in a medium bowl. Add the salad greens and toss to coat with the dressing. Divide the greens between 2 plates. Top with the sliced oranges, nuggets of the goat cheese and the almonds before serving.

NOTE
To toast the almonds, place them in a single layer in a small nonstick skillet and set over medium heat. Cook, swirling the pan from time to time, until lightly toasted, about 5 minutes. Don't leave the almonds unattended while cooking—they can burn quickly.

SHRIMP BAKED in CHAMPAGNE BUTTER SAUCE

preparation time	·	20 minutes
cooking time	·	10–12 minutes
makes	·	2 servings

If you're looking for a simple yet ultradelicious way to prepare shrimp, it's hard to go wrong with this dish. The shrimp is topped with a quick-to-make, buttery, sparkling wine mixture and cooked briefly. All you have to do is wait for your guest to say "Mmm, yummy!"

ERIC'S OPTIONS
Make shrimp and scallop in champagne butter sauce by replacing 6 of the shrimp with 6 large scallops. Cooking time remains the same.

12	large shrimp	12
⅓ cup	champagne or sparkling white wine	75 mL
3 Tbsp	melted butter	45 mL
1 tsp	fresh lemon juice	5 mL
1	small garlic clove, minced	1
pinch	cayenne pepper	pinch
to taste	salt and freshly ground black pepper	to taste
2 tsp	chopped fresh parsley	10 mL

Preheat the oven to 425°F (220°C). Peel the shrimp, leaving the tail portion attached. Devein the shrimp by making a shallow cut along the length of the back of each shrimp and removing any dark material found inside. Rinse the shrimp in cold water; thoroughly pat dry. (The shrimp can be prepared to this point several hours in advance of serving; keep covered and refrigerated until needed.)

Place the shrimp in a shallow baking dish large enough to hold them in a single layer, with about a ½-inch (1 cm) space between each of them. Combine the champagne, butter, lemon juice, garlic and cayenne in a small bowl. Pour the mixture over the shrimp; season lightly with salt and pepper. Bake 10 to 12 minutes, or until the shrimp have turned pink and are slightly firm to the touch. Divide the shrimp and sauce between 2 heated plates, sprinkle with parsley and serve.

Pictured with Saffron Rice, page 38

SAFFRON RICE

preparation time · 5 minutes
cooking time · about 30 minutes
makes · 2 servings

Saffron gives this rice a beautiful golden hue. It's expensive, but a little goes a long way. You can buy it in small jars at most supermarkets.

ERIC'S OPTIONS
To complement the golden hue of the saffron, mix 2 tsp (10 mL) chopped fresh parsley into the rice just before serving.

½ tsp	saffron threads	2 mL
¼ cup	boiling water	60 mL
1 Tbsp	olive oil	15 mL
1	small shallot, finely chopped	1
¾ cup	long-grain white rice	175 mL
1¼ cups	chicken stock or water	310 mL
to taste	salt and ground white pepper	to taste

Steep the saffron in the ¼ cup (60 mL) boiling water for 10 minutes. Heat the oil in a small pot over medium-high heat. Add the shallot and cook 1 minute. Add the rice and cook, stirring, 1 minute more. Add the steeped saffron and its liquid, stock, salt and pepper. Bring to a rapid boil, cover and then reduce the heat to its lowest setting. Cook the rice 15 minutes, or until tender.

ROAST BEEF TENDERLOIN
for TWO

preparation time	·	10 minutes
cooking time	·	25–30 minutes
makes	·	2 servings

The most tender cut of beef served with an easy-to-make red wine sauce. Because of the small size of this roast tenderloin, you will likely need to get a butcher to custom cut it for you.

ERIC'S OPTIONS

To make green peppercorn sauce, add 1 tsp (5 mL) green peppercorns to the skillet when reducing the wine. Green peppercorns are sold in small tins or jars at most supermarkets and fine food stores.

1½ Tbsp	olive oil	22.5 mL
1 lb	beef tenderloin roast	500 g
to taste	coarse sea salt and freshly ground black pepper	to taste
1 cup	beef stock	250 mL
1 Tbsp	flour	15 mL
⅓ cup	richly flavored red wine, such as Cabernet Sauvignon	75 mL

Preheat the oven to 400°F (200°C). Heat the oil in an ovenproof skillet over medium-high heat. Season the beef with salt and pepper, place in the skillet and sear on all sides. Place the skillet in the oven and roast 20 minutes for rare to medium-rare beef, 25 minutes for medium-rare to medium. Transfer the beef to a plate, tent with foil and let rest while you make the sauce.

Place the stock and flour in a bowl and whisk to combine. Drain the excess fat from the skillet and set on the stovetop over medium-high heat. Add the wine to the skillet and cook until it's reduced by half. Pour in the stock/flour mixture, bring to a simmer and simmer until lightly thickened. Season the sauce with salt and pepper and set aside on low heat. Thinly slice the beef, arrange it on a small serving platter and drizzle with some of the sauce. Serve the remaining sauce in a small sauceboat alongside.

CORNISH HEN with RASPBERRY GINGER GLAZE

preparation time	·	15 minutes
cooking time	·	50 minutes
makes	·	2 servings

A Cornish game hen split in half makes two nice portions, and this rich red raspberry sauce spiked with fresh ginger glazes the bird perfectly.

ERIC'S OPTIONS
Make the glaze with another type of jam, such as blackberry or red currant. For added texture, sprinkle the hens with 2 tsp (10 mL) toasted sesame seeds after the second basting.

1	Cornish game hen	1
to taste	salt and freshly ground black pepper	to taste
⅓ cup	raspberry jam	75 mL
1 Tbsp	soy sauce	15 mL
1 Tbsp	balsamic vinegar	15 mL
1 Tbsp	water	15 mL
1 tsp	chopped fresh ginger	5 mL
¼ tsp	dried tarragon	1 mL

Preheat the oven to 375°F (190°C). With kitchen shears or a sharp knife, cut along both sides of the hen's backbone and remove the bone. Place the hen breast side up and press it flat. Cut it in half down the middle of the breastbone. Place the hen halves, skin side up, in a roasting pan; season with salt and pepper, and roast for 30 minutes.

While the hen roasts, place the jam, soy sauce, vinegar and water in a small saucepan. Bring to a simmer and stir until the jam is melted and well combined with the other ingredients. Strain the mixture through a fine sieve into a bowl. Mix in the ginger and tarragon. When the hen halves have roasted 30 minutes, baste with half the raspberry mixture. Roast 10 minutes longer, and then baste with the remaining glaze. Roast 10 minutes more, or until cooked through.

BANANAS FLAMBÉ with BOURBON and PECANS

preparation time · 10 minutes
cooking time · about 5–6 minutes
makes · 2 servings

This classic dessert is given a southern-US style by flambéing the bananas with bourbon, instead of rum or brandy, and accenting them with pecans, the only nut tree native to the United States.

ERIC'S OPTIONS
Sprinkle the bananas with toasted, sliced almonds instead of pecans.

1½ Tbsp	butter	22.5 mL
2 Tbsp	packed golden brown sugar	30 mL
1 Tbsp	orange juice	15 mL
1 Tbsp	fresh lime juice	15 mL
pinch	ground cinnamon	pinch
pinch	ground nutmeg	pinch
2	large bananas, peeled and quartered	2
1 oz	bourbon, warmed	30 mL
2 Tbsp	pecan pieces	30 mL
	vanilla ice cream	

Melt the butter in a small skillet over medium-high heat. Stir in the brown sugar and cook until the sugar melts. Add the orange and lime juice and cook, whisking, until a smooth, caramel-like sauce forms, about 1 minute. Mix in the cinnamon and nutmeg. Add the bananas and turn to coat. Add the bourbon, tilt the pan slightly away from you, and very carefully ignite with a long match. Cook until the flames die out, about 1 to 2 minutes. Sprinkle in the pecans. Serve the bananas warm over ice cream.

COOKING WITH ALCOHOL

Notwithstanding popular belief, cooking does not evaporate or burn off all the alcohol you add to a dish. Cooking time and the strength of the alcohol will determine how much of it is retained.

For example, when alcohol is added at the end of cooking, even if it's ignited and then removed from the heat, much of the alcohol will remain. If it's simmered for hours, such as in a braised meat dish, only a trace of alcohol will be left. The higher the alcohol content of the beverage you add, the greater the volume of alcohol will remain after cooking.

FRESH FRUIT SKEWERS with ORANGE YOGURT DIPPING SAUCE

preparation time	·	10 minutes
cooking time	·	none
makes	·	2 servings

I like to serve this light, colorful dessert after a rich and filling main course.

ERIC'S OPTIONS
Substitute your favorite fresh fruit, such as cubes of mango, halved fresh figs, and thickly sliced banana.

4	fresh strawberries, stems removed	4
4	1-inch (2.5 cm) cubes fresh pineapple	4
1	medium kiwi, peeled and quartered	1
1/3 cup	yogurt	75 mL
1 Tbsp	packed golden brown sugar	15 mL
1 Tbsp	fresh orange juice or orange liqueur	15 mL
2 tsp	chopped fresh mint	10 mL

Supper Group
18/1/14

very good

Assemble four 6-inch (15 cm) wooden skewers and thread a strawberry, a pineapple cube and a quarter of the kiwi on each. Arrange the skewers on a decorative plate. Combine the yogurt, brown sugar, orange juice or liqueur and mint in a small bowl. Set the bowl on the plate with the skewers. This can be prepared several hours in advance, wrapped and refrigerated until serving time.

DARK BELGIAN CHOCOLATE MOUSSE

preparation time	·	20 minutes
cooking time	·	a few minutes
makes	·	2 servings

14/2/10
By Stick
for
Valentines
Yummy!

Here's a rich-tasting, yet light-textured, chocolaty dessert that's infused with the taste of orange liqueur.

ERIC'S OPTIONS
The mousse can be made up to a day in advance. If you don't want to use alcohol, replace the orange liqueur with orange juice.

Double ←

¼ cup	whipping cream	60 mL
1 Tbsp	orange liqueur	15 mL
2 Tbsp	granulated sugar	30 mL
1	large egg, separated	1
2 oz	dark Belgian chocolate, coarsely chopped	60 g
2 Tbsp	whipping cream	30 mL
2	mint sprigs, for garnish	2

Whip the ¼ cup (60 mL) whipping cream in a small bowl until stiff peaks form. Cover and refrigerate. Place the orange liqueur, sugar and egg yolk in a medium bowl and whisk to combine. Place the chocolate in a small heatproof bowl set over, not in, a small pot of barely simmering water; stir until the chocolate melts. Slowly pour the melted chocolate into the liqueur mixture, whisking constantly.

Place the egg white in a small bowl and beat until stiff peaks form. Whisk one-third of the egg white into the chocolate mixture to lighten it, and then gently fold in the remainder. Fold the whipped cream into the chocolate/egg white mixture. Spoon into 2 small, decorative, 6 oz (175 mL) glasses. (A port or sherry style glass works well.) Cover and refrigerate 3 to 4 hours to set the mousse.

When ready to serve, whip the 2 Tbsp (30 mL) whipping cream in a small bowl until stiff peaks form. Dollop an equal amount of the whipped cream on each mousse. Garnish each with a mint sprig and serve.

MENUS

"BE MY VALENTINE?" DINNER

Here's a lovely meal for 2 that's designed to allow you to spend most of the evening with your loved one, as much of the preparation can be done well before you sit down. The canapés, chopped lettuce and walnuts for the salad, fruit skewers and dipping sauce can be prepared a few hours in advance and refrigerated—except for the walnuts, which should be kept at room temperature. The Cornish game hen can be split and refrigerated in the roasting pan until you're ready to put it in the oven. The glaze can also be readied ahead of time and refrigerated; just warm it to make it fluid again before using it. Serve the salad as a separate course or serve it alongside the hen. If you choose the former, serve the hens with Saffron Rice (page 38) and a steamed vegetable, such as a mix of broccoli and cauliflower florets.

- Heart-Shaped Smoked Salmon Canapés (page 29)
- Romaine Hearts with Roquefort Cheese and Candied Walnuts (page 33)
- Cornish Hen with Raspberry Ginger Glaze (page 40)
- Fresh Fruit Skewers with Orange Yogurt Dipping Sauce (page 43)

"WE'RE GETTING MARRIED!" DINNER

When I proposed to my wife at our apartment in Toronto many years ago, a special dinner along the lines of this menu soon followed. She worked that day and I was at home getting all the elements of the meal ready. The soup in this menu can be made earlier in the day, cooled, refrigerated and reheated just before serving. The croutons can also be baked ahead, cooled and stored at room temperature on a covered plate until needed. The shrimp, topped with the sauce, can be made oven ready up to an hour in advance of serving. The mousse can be made the day before the meal. I like to serve the succulent shrimp and saffron rice with steamed asparagus, sliced baguette and cool glasses of champagne or sparkling wine.

Continued on the next page . . .

- Roasted Red Pepper Soup with Heart-shaped Parmesan Croutons (page 30)
- Shrimp Baked in Champagne Butter Sauce (page 36)
- Saffron Rice (page 38)
- Dark Belgian Chocolate Mousse (page 44)

"HAPPY ANNIVERSARY" DINNER

An anniversary, whether it celebrates six fabulous months of dating or 20 wonderful years of marriage, is the perfect time to enjoy a fine meal together. Like the other menus in this chapter, some of the dishes can be readied ahead of time. The melts can be made oven-ready, and you can toast the almonds, slice the oranges and prepare the salad dressing a few hours in advance. Keep everything refrigerated, except the almonds. At dinnertime, sear the beef and let it sit at room temperature while you enjoy the first course of melts. Put the beef in the oven, and enjoy the salad while the beef cooks. Serve the beef with small, boiled new potatoes and buttered green beans.

- Portobello Mushroom and Camembert Melts (page 26)
- Mixed Salad Greens with Goat Cheese, Oranges and Almonds (page 35)
- Roast Beef Tenderloin for Two (page 39)
- Bananas Flambé with Bourbon and Pecans (page 41)

CELEBRATE SPRING!

CHAPTER THREE

FRUIT COCKTAIL with SPARKLING WINE

preparation time · 15 minutes
cooking time · none
makes · 6 servings

Light, bubbly and colorful—this easy-to-make fruit cocktail is always a hit at brunch. You may wish to have an extra bottle of sparkling wine on hand just in case you need to top up the glasses.

ERIC'S OPTIONS
To make this drink nonalcoholic, replace the wine with non-alcoholic, sparkling apple cider. You'll find this beverage in the juice aisle of many supermarkets.

1 cup	fresh or frozen blueberries	250 mL
1	medium banana, peeled and sliced	1
1	medium-sized ripe mango, peeled and cubed	1
12	medium strawberries, hulled and sliced	12
3	medium kiwis, peeled, halved lengthwise and sliced	3
1	24 oz (750 mL) bottle sparkling wine	1
6	mint sprigs for garnish	6

Divide the fruit equally among six 6 to 8 oz (175 to 250 mL) decorative glasses. Top with the sparkling wine. Garnish each serving with a mint sprig and serve with a spoon for scooping out the fruit.

SPARKLING
JUICE

preparation time · 5 minutes
cooking time · none
makes · 4 servings

This simple, refreshing drink with bubbles will start off your morning in fine fashion. Make sure all the fruit juices are well chilled before combining them. Sparkling nonalcoholic apple cider is available in the juice aisle of many supermarkets.

ERIC'S OPTIONS
Adult guests may wish to substitute sparkling wine for the nonalcoholic apple cider in this drink.

⅔ cup	orange juice	150 mL
⅔ cup	guava, pineapple or papaya juice	150 mL
⅔ cup	cranberry or pomegranate juice	150 mL
2 Tbsp	fresh lime juice	30 mL
2 cups	sparkling nonalcoholic apple cider	500 mL
4	lime wedges for garnish	4

Place the fruit juices in a jug and whisk to combine. Pour into 4 tall decorative glasses. Top up each glass with the sparkling cider. Garnish the rims with the lime wedges and serve.

CURRIED CARROT SOUP with MINTY YOGURT

	preparation time	·	15 minutes
	cooking time	·	25 minutes
	makes	·	4 servings

The humble carrot is the base of this very flavorful soup, accented with aromatic curry and fresh orange juice and topped with tangy yogurt and refreshing mint.

ERIC'S OPTIONS
This soup, without the yogurt and mint garnish, freezes well. If you have the time, double the recipe, cool what you don't need to room temperature and freeze it in a tightly sealed container. To serve, thaw in the refrigerator overnight. Reheat the next day and top with minty yogurt.

2 Tbsp	vegetable oil	30 mL
3	medium carrots, peeled and sliced	3
1	medium onion, halved and sliced	1
2 tsp	chopped fresh ginger	10 mL
2	garlic cloves, chopped	2
3 Tbsp	all-purpose flour	45 mL
2–3 tsp	mild curry powder	10–15 mL
4 cups	chicken or vegetable stock	1 L
½ cup	fresh orange juice	125 mL
2 tsp	grated orange zest	10 mL
to taste	salt and ground white pepper	to taste
⅓ cup	yogurt	75 mL
1 Tbsp	chopped fresh mint	15 mL
for garnish	small mint springs	for garnish

Place the oil in a pot over medium heat. When it's hot, add the carrot, onion, ginger and garlic and cook 3 to 4 minutes. Stir in the flour and curry powder and cook 2 minutes more. While stirring, slowly pour in stock. Mix in the orange juice and orange zest. Bring the soup to a simmer and cook until the carrots are very tender, about 15 minutes.

Purée the soup in a blender or food processor, or in the pot with an immersion blender. Return the soup to a simmer and season with salt and white pepper. Place the yogurt in a small bowl and mix in the chopped mint. Ladle the soup into bowls, place a spoonful of yogurt in the center of each and garnish with mint.

MIXED GREENS with TARRAGON RANCH DRESSING

preparation time	·	20 minutes
cooking time	·	none
makes	·	6 servings

This classic mayonnaise-based dressing, which is infused with the licorice-like taste of tarragon, enlivens the flavor of the crisp, raw vegetables in this colorful salad.

ERIC'S OPTIONS
You can substitute the baby salad greens with any greens, such as baby spinach or chopped romaine, leaf or head lettuce. Rather than tarragon, flavor the dressing with another type of fresh herb, such as dill or chives.

SALAD DRESSING

½ cup	mayonnaise	125 mL
½ cup	buttermilk	125 mL
1 Tbsp	fresh lemon juice	15 mL
2 tsp	Dijon mustard	10 mL
1	garlic clove, finely chopped	1
1 Tbsp	chopped fresh tarragon	15 mL
½ tsp	granulated sugar	2 mL
to taste	salt and ground white pepper	to taste

SALAD

10–12 cups	mixed baby salad greens	2.5–3 L
1	carrot, cut in half lengthwise and thinly sliced into strips	1
⅓	English cucumber, halved and sliced	⅓
8	radishes, thinly sliced	8
½	yellow bell pepper, cut into thin strips	½
2	green onions, thinly sliced	2

Whisk the dressing ingredients together. Cover and refrigerate until needed.

Place the salad ingredients in a decorative bowl and toss to combine, ensuring some of the sliced vegetables decorate the top. Serve the dressing alongside so diners can help themselves to the salad and dress it as desired.

CHILLED ASPARAGUS with CHERRY TOMATO BASIL VINAIGRETTE

preparation time · 10 minutes
cooking time · 2–3 minutes
makes · 8 servings

Although asparagus is now available year-round, nothing says "spring" quite like this vegetable. Lightly cooked and paired with bright red tomatoes, it adds a cheerful note to the table.

ERIC'S OPTIONS
You can prepare the vinaigrette and cook the asparagus a few hours in advance and refrigerate. When it's almost time to serve, warm the vinaigrette to room temperature before spooning it over the asparagus.

2 lb	asparagus, tough lower parts of the stems trimmed and discarded	1 kg
⅓ cup	olive oil	75 mL
1 tsp	Dijon mustard	5 mL
2 Tbsp	red wine vinegar	30 mL
pinch	granulated sugar	pinch
to taste	salt and freshly ground black pepper	to taste
10–12	cherry tomatoes, finely chopped	10–12
2 Tbsp	chopped fresh basil	30 mL

Bring a large pot of water to a boil. Add the asparagus and boil until bright green and crisp/tender, about 2 to 3 minutes. Drain well, then plunge the asparagus into ice-cold water to stop the cooking. Drain well, dry on a kitchen towel and arrange on a platter.

Place the oil, mustard, vinegar, sugar, salt and pepper in a medium bowl and whisk to combine. Mix in the tomatoes and basil. Spoon the vinaigrette over the asparagus. Allow the flavors to meld at room temperature for 15 to 20 minutes before serving.

SPINACH SALAD with STRAWBERRIES and WALNUTS

preparation time · 10 minutes
cooking time · 10 minutes
makes · 6 servings

Welcome spring with this fresh-tasting, colorful salad of bright green spinach, sweet red berries, rich nuts and creamy cheese. The sweet and tangy flavor of balsamic vinegar in the dressing helps to tame the earthy taste of the spinach, which tends to make even those who don't care for this leafy green a fan of this salad.

ERIC'S OPTIONS
Instead of just strawberries, toss this salad with a mix of fresh berries, such as sliced strawberries and whole blueberries, raspberries and blackberries. For the baby spinach, substitute baby salad greens or chopped or torn leaf lettuce.

2 Tbsp	balsamic vinegar	30 mL
3 Tbsp	extra virgin olive oil	45 mL
1 tsp	Dijon mustard	5 mL
2 tsp	honey	10 mL
to taste	salt and freshly ground black pepper	to taste
1	5 oz (150 g) bag or box baby spinach, washed and dried	1
½ lb	fresh strawberries, hulled and sliced	250 g
⅓ cup	walnuts	75 mL
¼ lb	blue or soft goat cheese, pulled into small nuggets	125 g

Place the vinegar, oil, mustard, honey, salt and pepper in a salad bowl and whisk to combine. Add the spinach, strawberries, walnuts and cheese, and toss to coat, ensuring some of the strawberries, walnuts and cheese decorate the top, and serve.

MAKE-AHEAD
EGGS BENEDICT

preparation time	·	40 minutes
cooking time	·	about 25 minutes
makes	·	6 servings (2 eggs each)

Preparing eggs Benedict for a table full of guests can be a challenge if you are trying to poach the eggs, toast the English muffins and make the hollandaise sauce all at the last minute. This recipe allows you to spread out those tasks. You can softly poach the eggs in advance, make the sauce 30 minutes before it's needed, and quickly toast the muffins on a baking sheet under the broiler. When you're ready to serve, it's a simple matter of assembling the bacon, eggs and sauce on the muffins and making it all piping hot in the oven.

ERIC'S OPTIONS
To make this with smoked salmon and spinach, replace each slice of back bacon with 1 to 2 slices of smoked salmon. Top each muffin with ¼ cup (60 mL) wilted fresh spinach, drained of excess moisture. Continue with the eggs, hollandaise sauce and baking as described in the recipe.

2 tsp	white vinegar	10 mL
12	large eggs	12
3	large egg yolks	3
¼ cup	white wine	60 mL
½ cup	butter, melted	125 mL
to taste	white pepper	to taste
dash	Tabasco sauce, Worcestershire sauce and fresh lemon juice	dash
6	English muffins	6
12	slices Canadian (back) bacon	12
1 Tbsp	finely chopped fresh parsley	15 mL

Bring a large, wide pot of water to a gentle simmer. Add the vinegar. Fill a large bowl with ice-cold water. Swirl the simmering water with a spoon, and then crack 3 to 4 of the eggs into the water. (The movement of the water will help prevent the eggs from touching.) Poach the eggs 2 minutes; the yolks should still be quite soft. With a large, slotted spoon, carefully lift the eggs out of the water and place in the bowl of ice-cold water. This will stop the cooking and cool the eggs. Repeat these steps with the remaining eggs. Carefully lift the eggs out of the cold water and set on a large plate covered with plastic wrap or parchment paper. (The eggs can be prepared to this point several hours in advance, or even the night before. Cover and refrigerate until needed.)

Place the egg yolks in a heatproof bowl; whisk in the wine. Place the bowl over a pot of simmering water. Vigorously and rapidly whisk until the egg yolks become very light and thickened and feel warm, not hot. (This will occur quite quickly; do not overcook or the egg yolks will scramble.) Remove from the heat and slowly whisk in the melted butter, a few dribbles at a time. When the butter is all incorporated, season the hollandaise with white pepper, Tabasco, Worcestershire and lemon juice. Cover the bowl with plastic wrap and set aside until needed.

Preheat the broiler. Cut or split the English muffins in half and set, cut side up, on a large baking sheet. Broil the muffins until lightly toasted; remove from the oven and set aside. Preheat the oven to 425°F (220°C). Transfer the muffins to a parchment paper–lined baking sheet. Place a slice of bacon on each muffin half. Set a poached egg on top of the bacon. Top the eggs with the hollandaise sauce. Bake for 12 to 15 minutes, or until the eggs are heated through and the hollandaise sauce is lightly golden. Divide among plates, sprinkle with parsley and serve.

HISTORY OF EGGS BENEDICT

According to a number of sources, eggs Benedict was created at Delmonico's Restaurant around 1894. This Manhattan eatery was the birthplace of many famous dishes, such as Delmonico steak, lobster Newburg and baked Alaska. The story goes that one day, regular lunch customers Mr. and Mrs. LeGrand Benedict wanted to try something new. Mrs. Benedict and the restaurant's maître d' discussed the possibilities, and the dish now known as eggs Benedict was the result of their culinary conversation. With its base of crisp bread topped with succulent, smoky meat and a perfectly poached egg, all covered with a silky sauce, you can understand why it was a hit with the Benedicts and became a classic dish that remains popular today.

SCRAMBLED EGGS with HAVARTI and CHIVES

preparation time · 10 minutes
cooking time · 4–5 minutes
makes · 4 servings

This quick egg dish is rich with creamy havarti cheese and sprinkled with one of the first fresh herbs you'll see in backyard gardens in the spring, chives.

ERIC'S OPTIONS
For added protein, if you're not serving the eggs with a breakfast meat, mix 1 cup (250 mL) of cubed ham into the beaten eggs before cooking.

8	large eggs	8
⅓ cup	milk	75 mL
¼ lb	havarti cheese, cut into small cubes	125 g
to taste	salt and freshly ground black pepper	to taste
3 Tbsp	butter	45 mL
1 Tbsp	snipped fresh chives	15 mL

Place the eggs in a medium-sized bowl and beat until the yolks and whites are thoroughly combined. Mix in the milk, cheese, salt and pepper. Melt the butter in a large nonstick skillet over medium heat, and then add the egg mixture. As it begins to set on the bottom, gently move a heatproof spatula across the bottom and sides of the skillet to form large, soft curds. Continue cooking until the eggs are still moist but there is no visible liquid egg remaining. Spoon into a serving dish, sprinkle with the chives and serve.

RAINBOW FRUIT SKEWERS with MAPLE-SWEETENED WHIPPED CREAM

preparation time · 15 minutes
cooking time · none
makes · 4 servings

A fine mix of fresh fruit will create a rainbow of color and good taste when threaded together on a skewer.

ERIC'S OPTIONS
For a lighter option, serve the fruit with thick yogurt (instead of whipped cream) that has been sweetened (to taste) with maple syrup.

24–32	assorted slices, chunks or small, whole pieces of fruit, such as mango, date, apple, banana, kiwi, grape, grapefruit, strawberry or orange	24–32
4	wooden or metal skewers	4
	fresh lemon juice, if needed	
½ cup	whipping cream	125 mL
2 Tbsp	maple syrup	30 mL

Thread 6 to 8 different types of fresh fruit on each skewer. If using fruit such as apples or pears, brush the cut sides of them lightly with lemon juice before skewering to prevent oxidation.

Whip the cream until soft peaks form. Add the maple syrup and beat until stiff peaks form. Serve the whipped cream in a bowl alongside the skewers and allow your guests to dollop some on their plates, for dipping the fruit into.

APPLE-GLAZED BREAKFAST SAUSAGES

preparation time · 5 minutes
cooking time · about 10 minutes
makes · 4 servings

After browning, the sausages are simmered in apple juice or cider until the liquid cooks down and becomes a sweet glaze.

ERIC'S OPTIONS
To make maple-glazed sausages, omit the apple juice or cider and cook the sausages entirely through in the skillet. Drain the excess fat. Drizzle the sausages with 2 Tbsp (30 mL) maple syrup. Roll the sausages around in the pan to coat them with the syrup and serve.

1 Tbsp	vegetable oil	15 mL
12	pork, turkey or chicken breakfast sausages	12
⅓ cup	apple juice or cider	75 mL

Heat the oil in a large skillet over medium to medium-high heat. Add the sausages and cook until nicely browned on all sides, about 5 minutes. Discard the excess fat. Add the juice or cider to the skillet, bring to a simmer and cook until the sausages are cooked through and the juice or cider has almost evaporated and nicely glazed the sausages.

SWEET BELL PEPPER HASH BROWNS

preparation time · 20 minutes
cooking time · 10–13 minutes
makes · about 6–8 servings

To save time in the morning the potatoes can be parboiled the night before, cooled on a tray, covered and refrigerated. The red and green peppers give these potatoes a great taste and a festive look.

ERIC'S OPTIONS
For a meaty taste, add ½ cup (125 mL) finely chopped corned beef to the potatoes when first starting to fry them.

2 lb	white-skinned potatoes	1 kg
3 Tbsp	vegetable oil	45 mL
½	medium onion, finely chopped	½
½	red bell pepper, finely chopped	½
½	green bell pepper, finely chopped	½
¼ tsp	paprika	1 mL
½ tsp	ground cumin	2 mL
to taste	salt and freshly ground black pepper to taste	

Cut the potatoes, unpeeled, into ½-inch (1 cm) cubes and gently boil until just tender and still holding their shape, about 4 to 5 minutes. Drain the potatoes well. Heat the oil in a very large skillet over medium heat. Add the potatoes, onion, red and green bell pepper, paprika and cumin and cook 6 to 8 minutes, or until the potatoes are nicely crusted and colored. Season with salt and pepper and serve.

BAKED SALMON with CREAMY SHRIMP SAUCE

preparation time · 20 minutes
cooking time · 15–18 minutes
makes · 8 servings

Decadently delicious, this seafood dish will feed a table full of guests and cooks up in less than 20 minutes.

ERIC'S OPTIONS
Halibut fillets are equally good in this recipe. Vary the sauce by replacing the shrimp with an equal amount of crabmeat, or use a mix of shrimp and crab.

8	5 oz (150 g) salmon fillets	8
3 Tbsp	melted butter	45 mL
to taste	salt and white pepper	to taste
½ cup	white wine	125 mL
2	garlic cloves, crushed	2
1 tsp	dried tarragon	5 mL
½ tsp	paprika	2 mL
2 cups	whipping cream	500 mL
½ lb	small cooked salad shrimp	250 g
2	green onions, thinly sliced	2

Preheat the oven to 350°F (180°C). Line a baking sheet with parchment paper. Arrange the salmon in a single layer skin side down. Brush the fish with the melted butter; season with salt and pepper. Bake the salmon for 15 to 18 minutes, or until cooked through.

While the fish bakes, place the wine, garlic, tarragon and paprika in a medium-sized pot and bring to a simmer. Simmer until the wine has reduced by half. Add the cream and bring back to a simmer. Continue cooking until the mixture lightly thickens. Stir in the shrimp and heat them through for a few minutes. Season the sauce with salt and pepper. Keep the sauce warm over low heat.

When the salmon is cooked, place on individual serving plates and top with the sauce. Sprinkle with green onions and serve.

GRILLED CHICKEN BREAST with SMOKED HAM and BRIE

preparation time · 10 minutes
cooking time · 8–10 minutes
makes · 4 servings

This dish is similar to Chicken Cordon Bleu, where tender chicken, smoky ham and lovely cheese come together in one dish. However, in this combination of those tastes, the chicken is grilled, not breaded and fried, making it lighter-tasting and perfect for a spring lunch.

ERIC'S OPTIONS
If you like creamy blue-veined cheese, replace the brie with slices of Cambozola or Gorgonzola cheese.

4	6 oz (175 g) boneless, skinless chicken breasts	4
2 Tbsp	vegetable oil	30 mL
to taste	salt and freshly ground black pepper	to taste
8	shaved slices smoked ham (see Note)	8
4	slices brie cheese, about ¼ inch (6 mm) thick and 5 inches (12 cm) long	4
2 tsp	chopped fresh parsley	10 mL

Preheat your barbecue to medium-high. Brush the chicken with the oil; season with salt and pepper. Grill the chicken 3 to 4 minutes per side, or until just cooked through. Lower the heat on the barbecue to low. Top each piece of chicken with 2 slices of ham. Top the ham with a slice of brie. Close the lid of the barbecue for a few minutes, until the cheese just begins to melt but still hold its shape. Transfer the chicken to plates, sprinkle with parsley and serve.

NOTE
Most supermarkets sell smoked ham in their in-store delicatessens.

HAM GLAZED with HONEY, MUSTARD and SPICE

preparation time · 15 minutes
cooking time · 1 hour 55 minutes
makes · 10–12 servings

It's hard to go wrong with a baked glazed ham. It's easy to cook because the ham sold in supermarkets, unless it's labeled as fresh raw ham, is fully cooked and simply needs to be heated through. This is where you can add your own tasty glazing. After the meal, there always seem to be some leftovers for making tasty sandwiches.

ERIC'S OPTIONS
Instead of honey, use an equal amount of maple syrup in the glazing mixture.

6–7 lb	bone-in, shank portion ham (see Note)	2.7–3.15 kg
⅓ cup	liquid honey, warmed	75 mL
3 Tbsp	Dijon mustard	45 mL
1 tsp	pure vanilla extract	5 mL
½ tsp	ground cinnamon	2 mL
¼ tsp	ground nutmeg	1 mL
¼ tsp	ground cloves	1 mL

Preheat the oven to 325°F (160°C). Trim the ham of any tough outer skin and some of the excess fat, leaving a thin layer of the latter intact. Score the top of the ham in a diamond pattern, making shallow cuts 1 inch (2.5 cm) apart. Place the ham in a roasting pan and bake for 75 minutes. While the ham bakes, combine the honey, mustard, vanilla, cinnamon, nutmeg and cloves in a bowl.

When the ham has baked 75 minutes, brush it with half of the glaze and bake 20 minutes longer. Brush with the remaining glaze and bake a further 20 minutes. Remove from the oven, loosely cover with foil and let it rest for 10 to 15 minutes before carving it into thin slices.

NOTE
Ham comes from the back leg of the pig and often is cut into the shank portion (the lower part of the leg) and the hip portion (the upper part of the leg). I prefer the shank portion as it's meatier and easier to carve.

ROAST LEG of LAMB with MINT PESTO CRUST

preparation time · 25 minutes
cooking time · depends on desired doneness
makes · 8 servings

There's no mint jelly in this updated version of roast lamb. Instead, the juicy meat is lusciously crusted and flavored with mint pesto—a rich, forest-green paste made by puréeing fresh mint with olive oil, garlic, Parmesan cheese and pine nuts.

ERIC'S OPTIONS
For a quicker and easier-to-make pesto, mix 1 cup (250 mL) of store-bought basil pesto in a bowl with ¼ cup (60 mL) chopped fresh mint. Thin the pesto with a little extra virgin olive oil if too thick.

1½ cups	loosely packed fresh mint leaves	375 mL
½ cup	pine nuts	125 mL
⅓ cup	freshly grated Parmesan cheese	75 mL
½ cup	extra virgin olive oil	125 mL
4	medium garlic cloves, sliced	4
1	5–7 lb (2.2–3.15 kg) leg of lamb	1
to taste	coarse sea salt and freshly ground black pepper	to taste
¼ cup	breadcrumbs	60 mL
3 cups	beef stock	750 mL

Preheat the oven to 450°F (230°C). Place the mint, pine nuts, cheese, oil and garlic in a food processor and pulse until well combined. Place the lamb, fatty side up, in a large, shallow roasting pan. Spread the pesto on the top and sides of the lamb. Sprinkle with the salt, pepper and breadcrumbs. Roast the lamb for 20 minutes, and then reduce the heat to 325°F (160°C) and cook to the desired doneness (see Lamb Roasting Guide on the facing page). Set the lamb on a platter, tent with foil and let it rest for 15 minutes.

While the lamb rests, make jus to serve with it. Remove excess fat from the roasting pan, place the pan on the stovetop and pour in the beef stock. Bring to a simmer, scraping the bottom of the pan to get the brown bits off the bottom; simmer 5 minutes.

Carve the lamb and arrange the meat on a warmed platter. Serve the jus in a sauceboat for drizzling on top of the meat.

LAMB ROASTING GUIDE

The roasting times below factor in the 15 minutes the lamb rests to set the juices after it's removed from the oven, during which time the lamb continues to cook. Because lamb legs can vary in thickness, an instant-read meat thermometer, sold at most stores selling kitchenware, is the best tool to use to gauge doneness. Insert it into the center of the thickest part of the leg to gauge how the lamb is progressing.

Rare
Allow 20 minutes per pound (500 g). Internal temperature of the lamb should be 125 to 130°F (50 to 55°C) before you remove it from the oven.

Medium rare
Allow 20 to 25 minutes per pound (500 g). Internal temperature should be 130 to 135°F (55 to 57°C) before you remove it from the oven.

Medium
Allow 25 minutes per pound (500 g). Internal temperature should be 140°F (60°C) before you remove it from the oven.

Well done
Allow 30 minutes per pound (500 g). Internal temperature should be 150°F (65°C) before you remove it from the oven.

How to carve a whole leg of lamb
If the meat has been tied with string, remove it after the lamb has rested. Make sure the leg is sitting on your cutting board fat side up. Insert a meat fork into the narrow, shank end of the leg and lift the lamb up at a 45-degree angle away from you. Using a sharp, thin carving knife, cut the meat into thin slices starting at the thicker, hip end of the leg. If your butcher has not removed the hip, or hitch bone, from the leg, you will have to make the slices more parallel to the leg bone. Continue slicing until you reach the joint where the lower and upper leg bones meet. Carefully move up the leg and cut thin slices from the shank end of the leg, where the meat is quite succulent. Turn the leg over and slice the meat from that side of the leg.

WARM RED and WHITE POTATO SALAD

preparation time · 25 minutes
cooking time · about 20 minutes
makes · 8 servings

This warm potato salad goes great with just about any roast. When the meat is done, you can quickly heat the potatoes in the oven while the meat rests.

ERIC'S OPTIONS
Use all red potatoes or all white potatoes, instead of a mix. For added texture, try whole grain Dijon mustard in place of the smooth variety. Instead of the green onions, sprinkle the potato salad with 2 or 3 Tbsp (30 or 45 mL) of snipped chives.

1¼ lb	small red-skinned potatoes, thickly sliced (unpeeled)	625 g
1¼ lb	small white-skinned potatoes, thickly sliced (unpeeled)	625 g
1 cup	grated carrots	250 mL
3	green onions, thinly sliced	3
1 tsp	finely grated lemon zest	5 mL
3 Tbsp	fresh lemon juice	45 mL
2 tsp	Dijon mustard	10 mL
½ tsp	granulated sugar	2 mL
to taste	salt and freshly ground black pepper	to taste
½ cup	olive oil	125 mL

Gently boil the potatoes until just tender and drain well. Arrange in a layer (with the potatoes overlapping slightly) on a large baking sheet and cool to room temperature. Sprinkle with the carrot and green onion. (The potatoes can be prepared to this point a few hours in advance; cover and refrigerate until needed.) Preheat the oven to 350°F (180°C). Combine the lemon zest, lemon juice, mustard, sugar, salt, pepper and olive oil in a bowl; spoon over the potatoes. Bake 10 to 12 minutes, or until the potatoes are well heated through. Spoon into a decorative dish and serve.

FAMILY-SIZED
RHUBARB CRISP

preparation time · 20 minutes
cooking time · 45 minutes
makes · 8–10 servings

This traditional family dessert is given a lift with the addition of orange juice and ginger. A scoop of vanilla ice cream or a dollop of whipped cream makes it even better.

ERIC'S OPTIONS

Instead of ground ginger, flavor the rhubarb filling with ¼ to ⅓ cup (60 to 75 mL) finely chopped candied ginger, which is sold at most supermarkets. It will add a sweet and spicy taste to the rhubarb filling.

NOTE

If using fresh rhubarb, you'll need about 10 medium-sized stalks to get the 10 cups (2.5 L) required for this recipe. Cut it into slices about ¾ inch (2 cm) thick.

FILLING

10 cups	sliced fresh or frozen rhubarb	2.5 L
1 cup	granulated sugar	250 mL
1 cup	orange juice	250 mL
1 cup	water	250 mL
2 Tbsp	fresh lemon juice	30 mL
2 tsp	cornstarch	10 mL
1 tsp	pure vanilla extract	5 mL
½ tsp	ground ginger	2 mL

TOPPING

2½ cups	rolled oats	625 mL
½ cup	packed golden brown sugar	125 mL
½ cup	butter, softened	125 mL
3 Tbsp	all-purpose flour	45 mL
1 tsp	ground cinnamon	5 mL
¼ tsp	ground nutmeg	1 mL

Mix the filling ingredients in a large bowl until well combined. Spoon into a 9- × 13-inch (3.5 L) baking dish. Set an oven rack in the middle position. Preheat the oven to 350°F (180°C). Place the topping ingredients in a medium bowl. Mix well with your fingertips to combine the butter with the other ingredients. Sprinkle the topping evenly over the filling. Bake for 45 minutes, until golden brown and bubbling.

LEMON LOVER'S CUPCAKES

preparation time ·	30 minutes
cooking time ·	20–25 minutes
makes ·	18 cupcakes

Lemon zest, lemon juice, lemon glaze and a lemon candy—this is definitely the cupcake for lemon lovers!

ERIC'S OPTIONS

Make orange-flavored cupcakes by replacing the lemon juice, lemon zest and lemon candies with orange juice, orange zest and orange candies.

CUPCAKES

½ cup	butter, softened	125 mL
1½ cups	granulated sugar	375 mL
1 Tbsp	grated lemon zest	15 mL
1 tsp	pure vanilla extract	5 mL
4	large eggs	4
½ cup	fresh lemon juice	125 mL
⅓ cup	milk	75 mL
2 cups	all-purpose flour	500 mL
1 Tbsp	baking powder	15 mL
½ tsp	salt	2 mL

GLAZE

2 Tbsp	fresh lemon juice	30 mL
⅓ cup	icing sugar	75 mL
18	jelly lemon candy slices	18
18	small mint sprigs (optional)	18

Continued on page 72 . . .

Continued on page 72 . . .

Preheat the oven to 350°F (180°C). Line one 12-cup muffin pan, and 6 cups of another muffin pan with paper liners. Place the butter, sugar, lemon zest and vanilla in a bowl and beat until well combined and lightened, about 3 to 4 minutes. Beat in the eggs one at a time. Mix in the lemon juice and milk. Whisk the flour, baking powder and salt together in a second bowl. Gradually mix the flour mixture into the egg mixture until just combined.

Spoon the batter into the baking cups. Bake for 20 to 25 minutes, or until puffed and golden and the top of a cupcake springs back when gently touched in the center. Cool the cupcakes on a baking rack to room temperature before removing them from the pan.

To make the glaze, place the lemon juice in a bowl. Whisk in the icing sugar very gradually, stirring constantly to form a smooth mixture. Spread on the tops of the cupcakes. Decorate the top of each cupcake with a lemon candy slice. Let the glaze set. Tent the cupcakes with plastic wrap until ready to serve; can be made up to a day before serving. When ready to serve, arrange the cupcakes on a serving tray and, if desired, garnish each with a small sprig of mint.

COCOA PAVLOVA with ORANGE-SCENTED STRAWBERRIES

preparation time	·	30 minutes
cooking time	·	90 minutes plus oven cooling time
makes	·	8 servings

Light, chocolaty, fruity and very impressive—and the meringue can be made ahead of time!

ERIC'S OPTIONS
Instead of just strawberries, top the meringue with a mix of sliced and whole fresh fruit, such as kiwi, mango, blueberries, raspberries and passion fruit.

4	large egg whites, at room temperature	4
½ tsp	cream of tartar	2 mL
1 cup	extra fine (berry) sugar (see Note next page)	250 mL
2 Tbsp	cocoa powder	30 mL
1 Tbsp	cornstarch	15 mL
1 tsp	pure vanilla extract	5 mL
1 lb	fresh strawberries, hulled and sliced	500 g
2–3 tsp	finely grated orange zest	10–15 mL
2 Tbsp	orange liqueur or fresh orange juice	30 mL
4 Tbsp	icing sugar	60 mL
1 cup	whipping cream	250 mL

Preheat the oven to 250°F (120°C). Line a baking sheet with parchment paper. Draw a 9-inch-diameter (23 cm) circle on the parchment. I use a 9-inch (23 cm) round cake pan as a guide.

Beat the egg whites and cream of tartar in a large stainless bowl with an electric beater, or in the bowl of your stand mixer, until very soft peaks form. Gradually add the extra fine sugar, whipping constantly, until all is incorporated. Keep whipping until the mixture is thick and glossy and stiff peaks form. Whip in the cocoa, cornstarch and vanilla until well combined.

Spoon the meringue to fit inside the circle drawn on the paper; build up the sides and make a shallow depression in the middle. Bake for 1½ hours. Turn off the heat and let the meringue cool in the oven for 3 hours. (The meringue can be made up to a day in advance. Store it in a tightly sealed container at room temperature.)

Place the strawberries, orange zest, orange liqueur or juice and 2 Tbsp (30 mL) of the icing sugar in a bowl and gently toss to combine. Cover and let the strawberries macerate at room temperature for 20 minutes.

Whip the cream until soft peaks form. Sweeten with the remaining 2 Tbsp (30 mL) icing sugar and beat until stiff peaks form. Spread the whipped cream in the center of the meringue, leaving a 1-inch (2.5 cm) border at the outer edge. Artfully arrange the strawberries on top of the whipped cream. Drizzle with any juices left in the bowl. Serve immediately.

NOTE
The finely granulated texture of extra fine (berry) sugar means it dissolves easily, which is why it's great for meringues. It's sold in small bags at most supermarkets.

MENUS

This spring brunch is full of color and vibrant tastes, a perfect match for this bright time of year. The recipes can be partially readied in advance and quickly finished off when needed, even the eggs Benedict. The recipes serve 6 but could easily be expanded for a larger group.

- Fruit Cocktail with Sparkling Wine (page 48)
- Make-Ahead Eggs Benedict (page 56)
- Sweet Bell Pepper Hash Browns (page 61)
- Baby Spinach Salad with Strawberries and Walnuts (page 55)

EASTER DINNER

This menu, which serves 8, features two brilliant-looking salads, one served warm and one served cold. Both can be readied in advance, which allows more time to focus on the main dish, which in this menu could be lamb, salmon or ham. If you choose the crisp for dessert, bake it while enjoying the main course.

- Roast Leg of Lamb with Mint Pesto Crust (page 66); Baked Salmon with Creamy Shrimp Sauce (page 62); or Ham Glazed with Honey, Mustard and Spice (page 65)
- Chilled Asparagus with Cherry Tomato Basil Vinaigrette (page 53)
- Warm Red and White Potato Salad (page 68)
- Lemon Lover's Cupcakes (page 70) or Family-Sized Rhubarb Crisp (page 69)

MOTHER'S DAY BREAKFAST

It's traditional in many families to make breakfast for Mom on Mother's Day. But this can be a challenge if she's the one who normally does the cooking. This tasty breakfast menu for 4 could save the day—it's quite easy to prepare, the kids can help and some of the work can be done in advance.

Continued on the next page . . .

Before starting with the hot food preparation, get the kids to set a beautiful table with a fresh tablecloth and napkins, flowers and nice plates. If you think Mom would enjoy a cup, brew a pot of coffee or tea to serve with the breakfast.

Brown the sausages as described in the recipe before cooking the eggs. Add the cider or juice to the skillet, start cooking the eggs, and both sausages and eggs should be ready around the same time. (If the sausages are done first, keep warm over low heat.) Meanwhile, the kids can make some toast to serve with the eggs, or, to make things simpler, serve the eggs with store-bought croissants, warmed in the oven a few minutes.

- Sparkling Juice (page 49)
- Rainbow Fruit Skewers with Maple-Sweetened Whipped Cream (page 59)
- Scrambled Eggs with Havarti and Chives (page 58)
- Apple-Glazed Breakfast Sausages (page 60)

MAY LONG WEEKEND SPRING LUNCH

If the May long weekend is the time you fire up the barbecue after winter dormancy, this lunch for 4 featuring grilled chicken is a perfect way to celebrate. The soup has a palate-awakening taste of spring mint, and you can prepare it up to a day in advance. Cover and refrigerate; when you're ready to serve, reheat, ladle it into bowls and garnish with the yogurt. For an attractive presentation of the main course, plate the chicken with the salad alongside. Serve the pavlova with a fine cup of tea or coffee, and/or, if desired, accent its flavors with a glass of orange liqueur or dessert wine.

- Curried Carrot Soup with Minty Yogurt (page 51)
- Grilled Chicken Breast with Smoked Ham and Brie (page 64)
- Mixed Greens with Tarragon Ranch Dressing (page 52)
- Cocoa Pavlova with Orange-Scented Strawberries (page 73)

SUMMER LONG WEEKENDS

CHAPTER FOUR

HOMEMADE LEMONADE with RASPBERRIES and MINT

preparation time · 10 minutes
cooking time · a few minutes
makes · 8–10 servings

The classic summer drink, dressed up with raspberries and mint.

ERIC'S OPTIONS

To make a summer cocktail, add 1½ oz (45 mL) vodka to each glass before adding the lemonade.

5 cups	cold water	1.25 L
1 cup	granulated sugar	250 mL
2 cups	freshly squeezed lemon juice (about 8–10 lemons)	500 mL
1–1½ cups	fresh raspberries	250–375 mL
for garnish	fresh mint sprigs	for garnish
	ice cubes	

Place 1 cup (250 mL) of the water in a small pot and bring to a boil over medium-high heat. Add the sugar and cook, stirring, until the sugar has completely dissolved and the liquid is clear, about 2 to 3 minutes. Remove from the heat, cool to room temperature and pour the mixture (called simple syrup) into an 8-cup (2 L) serving jug. Mix in the remaining 4 cups (1 L) of cold water and the lemon juice. Cover and refrigerate until needed. Can be made a day or two in advance of serving.

To serve, place 4 to 5 ice cubes in a glass, and drop in 5 to 6 raspberries and a mint sprig. Pour the lemonade and serve.

FRUITY ROSÉ SANGRIA

preparation time · 10 minutes
cooking time · none
makes · 12 servings

Shimmering, pale pink rosé makes a refreshing summer drink with this colorful mix of fresh fruit.

ERIC'S OPTIONS
If you're serving a smaller group, this recipe can easily be halved. For fizzy sangria, fill the glasses three-quarters full and top up with ice-cold soda water. Instead of rosé, make the sangria with red or white wine.

2	24 oz (750 mL) bottles dry rosé	2
½ cup	orange liqueur	125 mL
½ cup	icing sugar, or to taste	125 mL
4	medium-sized ripe apricots or plums, halved, pitted and thinly sliced	4
2	medium-sized ripe nectarines, halved, pitted and thinly sliced	2
32–40	fresh cherries, pitted, if desired	32–40
1 cup	fresh blueberries	250 mL
2	medium limes, halved and thinly sliced	2
	ice cubes	

Pour the wine and orange liqueur into a large bowl; whisk in the sugar until dissolved. Add the remaining ingredients except the ice cubes, cover and chill at least 4 hours, or overnight. To serve, fill a large pitcher half full with ice. Ladle in the sangria and serve, refilling the pitcher with more sangria and ice as needed.

TECHNICOLOR SUMMER SALSA

preparation time	·	30 minutes
cooking time	·	none
makes	·	4 cups (1 L)

I named this "Technicolor Salsa" because of the many colors—red, purple, yellow, orange and green—of the vegetables in it. Serve it as an appetizer with tortilla chips for dipping, or as a fresh and lively condiment for wraps, burgers and Mexican-style dishes, such as tacos and burritos.

ERIC'S OPTIONS
If you don't care for the taste of cilantro, mix 2 to 3 thinly sliced green onions into the salsa instead.

3	ripe medium tomatoes, finely chopped	3
1 cup	finely diced green zucchini	250 mL
½ cup	finely diced red onion	125 mL
½ cup	finely diced yellow bell pepper	125 mL
½ cup	finely diced orange bell pepper	125 mL
1	garlic clove, crushed	1
1	small to medium fresh jalapeño pepper, halved, seeds removed, flesh finely chopped	1
¼ cup	chopped fresh cilantro	60 mL
¼ cup	fresh lime juice	60 mL
1 tsp	ground cumin	5 mL
1 tsp	granulated sugar	5 mL
to taste	salt	to taste

Place all the ingredients in a bowl and gently toss to combine. Can be made a few hours in advance; cover and refrigerate until needed. Gently toss the salsa again just before serving.

Food and transportation

If your transportation to the picnic site is your feet or a bike, it's obviously wise to pack foods that are fairly light and compact. Foods that will nicely fit into a small cooler bag or backpack include cured meats, cheese, sliced baguette, nuts, fruit and fiber-filled cookies.

If you're traveling by car, you can pack a giant cooler full of stuff. However, the weight of the food can still be an issue if you have to haul the cooler quite a distance from where you park.

How to pack

Reserve cooler space for items that need to stay cold. To keep foods as cold as possible, pack well-chilled perishable foods in your cooler shortly before leaving for the picnic. Be sure you have plenty of icepacks to keep the food super-chilled. Place the food in the cooler in the order you'll eat it. That way the first item you'll serve will be right on top; you can grab it and quickly close the cooler to avoid warming up items you don't intend to eat until later in the day.

Accessories

Climatic conditions and the types of food and drink you're having will dictate what other items you'll need. Things to consider include plates, glasses, cutlery, serving utensils; napkins, a tablecloth and a picnic blanket; ice for drinks and a bottle opener; a small cutting board and knife; a cleaning cloth and garbage bags; and sunscreen and bug spray.

Leftover food

If you've been out all day, there's a good possibility any leftover perishable food, even if you put it back in your cooler, particularly on a hot day, will have warmed to a bacteria-building, unsafe temperature. When deciding if it is still safe to eat, remember this rule: when in doubt, throw it out.

ROASTED RED PEPPER HUMMUS

preparation time	·	10 minutes
cooking time	·	none
makes	·	about 2 cups (500 mL)

This red-hued version of the Greek-style dip is flavored with sweet and smoky-tasting roasted red pepper. Serve it as an appetizer with wedges of pita and raw vegetables, such as cucumber slices, carrot sticks and cauliflower florets.

ERIC'S OPTIONS

If you want to roast your own red pepper, place a large red bell pepper in a small baking pan lined with parchment paper. Roast at 375°F (190°C) for 30 minutes, turning once or twice, until the skin is blistered. Remove from the oven and cover the pan with foil. Let the pepper sit for 20 minutes. Uncover the pepper and slip the skin off. Cut the pepper in half, remove the seeds and it's ready to use.

1	19 oz (540 mL) can chickpeas	1
1	large roasted red pepper, coarsely chopped (see Note)	1
3–4 Tbsp	olive oil, plus some for drizzling	45–60 mL
3 Tbsp	tahini (see Note)	45 mL
2 Tbsp	fresh lemon juice, or to taste	30 mL
2	garlic cloves, coarsely chopped	2
2 tsp	ground cumin	10 mL
3 Tbsp	chopped fresh basil	45 mL
to taste	salt and freshly ground black pepper	to taste

Drain the chickpeas well, rinse with cold water, and drain well again. Place the chickpeas and the remaining ingredients in a food processor and pulse until smooth. Spoon the dip into a decorative bowl. The dip can be made a day or two in advance of serving; cover and refrigerate. Drizzle the hummus with a little olive oil before serving.

NOTE
Roasted red peppers and tahini, a paste made from sesame seeds, are available in jars at most supermarkets and Mediterranean-style delis.

Pictured with Fig and Olive Tapenade, page 86

FIG and OLIVE TAPENADE

preparation time	·	10 minutes
cooking time	·	15 minutes
makes	·	2 cups (500 mL)

I was inspired to create this recipe after a trip to California's Sonoma Valley, where foods such as tapenade are made with locally grown figs and olives. This Mediterranean-style spread and great summer appetizer is a wonderful combination of sweet figs nicely balanced with salty, sharp olives. Pine nuts, basil and other good things add even more rich flavor. I like to serve this tapenade with a creamy cheese, such as brie or goat cheese. The tastes mingle beautifully when combined on a slice of baguette or a cracker.

ERIC'S OPTIONS

To make a delicious canapé, spread toasted baguette rounds with a soft and creamy goat cheese. Top the cheese with a spoonful of tapenade. Garnish each canapé with a small, thin slice of pear and a small basil leaf.

NOTE

Dried black mission figs are available at many supermarkets and fine food stores in the same aisle as other bagged, dried fruits.

1 cup	dried black mission figs (see Note)	250 mL
1 cup	pitted kalamata olives	250 mL
¼ cup	pine nuts	60 mL
¼ cup	coarsely chopped basil	60 mL
¼ cup	extra virgin olive oil	60 mL
2 Tbsp	balsamic vinegar	30 mL
2	medium garlic cloves, chopped	2

Place the figs in a pot, cover with cold water and bring to a boil over high heat. Remove from the heat and let the figs plump up in the water for 15 minutes. Drain well and place the figs in a food processor. Add the remaining ingredients and pulse until well combined and finely chopped; do not purée. Transfer to a serving bowl, cover and refrigerate for 4 hours or overnight to allow the flavors to meld. (Refrigerated in a tightly sealed jar, the tapenade will keep for at least a week.) Serve the tapenade with slices of baguette or crackers to spread it on.

SHRIMP with PESTO
on GRILLED ZUCCHINI

preparation time · 25 minutes
cooking time · 2 minutes
makes · 18 pieces

Low in calories, zucchini makes a light but colorful base here for sweet, small shrimp dressed up with pesto and mayonnaise.

ERIC'S OPTIONS
For an even more colorful platter, make these with 9 slices of green zucchini and 9 slices of yellow.

7 oz	cooked salad shrimp, patted dry if thawed from frozen	200 g
2–3 Tbsp	mayonnaise	30–45 mL
1 Tbsp	store-bought or homemade pesto (see Pesto recipe, next page)	15 mL
to taste	salt and freshly ground black pepper	to taste
18	½-inch-thick (1 cm) slices of zucchini (about 1 medium)	18
2 Tbsp	olive oil	30 mL
18	small basil leaves, for garnish	18

Place the shrimp, mayonnaise, pesto, salt and pepper in a bowl and mix to combine. Cover and refrigerate until needed.

Preheat your grill to medium-high. Toss the zucchini with the oil and some salt and pepper. Grill the zucchini 1 minute per side, then arrange it on a platter and cool to room temperature. Top with the shrimp, garnish each bite with a basil leaf and serve.

PESTO

preparation time	·	5 minutes
cooking time	·	none
makes	·	1½ cups (375 mL)

Once prepared, refrigerate the pesto in a tightly sealed jar with a skim of olive oil on top for 1 to 2 weeks. You can also freeze it if you omit the Parmesan cheese, which does not do well in the freezer. I like to spoon it into ice-cube trays, freeze it solid, then unmold the cubes of pesto and keep them in a freezer bag. Beyond flavoring appetizers, the cubes of pesto can also be used to bolster the flavor of soups, sauces and pasta dishes.

ERIC'S OPTIONS

Make mixed herb pesto by replacing half of the basil with other herbs, such as parsley, mint or oregano. You can also experiment with the nuts you use, replacing the pine nuts with an equal amount of walnuts or toasted almonds.

4 cups	basil leaves, loosely packed	1 L
3–4	garlic cloves, coarsely chopped	3–4
½ cup	pine nuts	125 mL
½ cup	freshly grated Parmesan (optional)	125 mL
¾–1 cup	extra virgin olive oil	175–250 mL

Place the basil, garlic, pine nuts and Parmesan cheese, if using, in a food processor and pulse until coarsely chopped. Slowly add the oil and process until smooth. If you find the pesto too thick, add a little more oil.

CURRIED LAMB SKEWERS with MINT YOGURT

preparation time · 20 minutes plus marinating time
cooking time · about 4 minutes
makes · 24 skewers

Deep red, spice-filled, Indian-style curry paste is available in jars in the ethnic food aisle of most supermarkets. Choose from mild, medium or hot versions according to your preference. In this recipe, a small amount infuses a world of flavor into the lamb.

ERIC'S OPTIONS
Before grilling, set a double-thick strip of aluminum foil, the width of the non-meat-covered pieces of wood on each skewer, lengthwise on the front portion of the barbecue. Oil the uncovered bars of the grill. Set the lamb skewers on the grill so that the meat is over the flame, and the uncovered wood sits, protected, on the foil.

1½ lb	boneless lamb leg, cut into 24 thin strips	750 g
2 Tbsp	Indian-style curry paste	30 mL
2 Tbsp	fresh lime juice	30 mL
1 Tbsp	vegetable oil	15 mL
½ cup	thick yogurt	125 mL
2 Tbsp	chopped fresh mint	30 mL

Place the lamb, curry paste, lime juice and oil in a bowl and toss to combine. Cover and marinate in the refrigerator for 4 hours.

Soak 24 small wooden skewers in cold water for an hour or more. Combine the yogurt and mint in a bowl. Cover and refrigerate until needed.

Thread a piece of lamb on one end of each skewer. (The lamb can be prepared to this stage several hours in advance, covered and refrigerated. Warm at room temperature for 20 minutes before grilling.) Preheat your grill to medium-high. Lightly oil the bars of the grill. Grill the lamb 2 minutes per side, or until just cooked through. Arrange the skewers on a platter and serve the yogurt dipping sauce on the side.

CHERRY TOMATO and
GOAT CHEESE BRUSCHETTA

preparation time · 20 minutes
cooking time · 8–10 minutes
makes · 12 crostini

This is a completely simple and quickly made appetizer, but the textures and tastes of crisp, garlicky bread, creamy cheese and sweet cherry tomatoes make very flavorful bites. To create bite-sized bruschetta, choose a baguette that is about 1½ inches (4 cm) in diameter.

ERIC'S OPTIONS
For more color on the plate, use a mix of red and yellow cherry tomatoes. Yellow cherry tomatoes are available at some specialty food stores and farmers' markets.

12	¼-inch-thick (6 mm) slices of baguette	12
2 Tbsp	olive oil	30 mL
1	garlic clove, minced	1
¼ lb	soft goat cheese	125 g
4–6	cherry tomatoes, sliced	4–6
to taste	sea salt and freshly ground black pepper	to taste
12	small fresh basil leaves for garnish	12

Preheat the oven to 375°F (190°C). Place the slices of baguette on a baking sheet. Combine the oil and garlic in a small bowl and brush on the bread. Bake the bread until lightly toasted, about 8 to 10 minutes. Remove and cool to room temperature. (The toasted baguette slices can be made a few hours in advance; cover and store at room temperature.) Spread with the cheese. Top each bruschetta with 2 slices of cherry tomato. Sprinkle with salt and pepper. Garnish each crostini with a basil leaf and serve.

GREEN BEAN SALAD with TAHINI DRESSING

preparation time	·	10 minutes
cooking time	·	2 minutes
makes	·	6 servings

I came up with this idea after wondering what to do with the tahini I had left over from making hummus. Tahini, a tasty paste with a peanut butter–like consistency, is made from ground sesame seeds. It turns out that it makes a nice base for a salad dressing too, such as the citrus-flavored one adorning the green beans in this salad.

ERIC'S OPTIONS
If you'll be serving these beans at a picnic (see menu on page 113), put the blanched beans in a wide, shallow container, and the dressing and zest in separate, small containers and pack them in your cooler. When it's time to serve, drizzle the beans with the dressing, garnish with zest and serve.

¼ cup	tahini	60 mL
¼ cup	orange juice	60 mL
1 Tbsp	fresh lemon juice	15 mL
2 Tbsp	chopped fresh mint	30 mL
1	small garlic clove, crushed	1
pinch	ground cumin	pinch
to taste	salt and freshly ground black pepper	to taste
1¼ lb	green beans, trimmed and blanched (see Note)	625 g
for garnish	twirls of lemon zest	for garnish

Place the tahini, orange and lemon juice, mint, garlic, cumin, salt and pepper in a small bowl and mix well to combine. Arrange the beans on a platter. Drizzle with the tahini dressing. Garnish with the lemon zest and serve.

NOTE
To blanch the beans, cook in boiling water 2 minutes. Drain well, plunge into ice-cold water to chill them and then drain well again.

MAC and CHEESE SALAD

preparation time	·	20 minutes
cooking time	·	7–8 minutes
makes	·	8 servings

Here's a creamy and "cool" version of the always-popular combination of macaroni and cheese.

ERIC'S OPTIONS

For extra protein and a smoky taste, add ⅓ lb (170 g) ham or smoked turkey cut into small cubes.

1½ cups	elbow macaroni	375 mL
½ cup	mayonnaise	125 mL
¼ cup	sour cream	60 mL
2 Tbsp	regular or whole grain Dijon mustard	30 mL
1 Tbsp	finely chopped fresh sage (or 1 tsp/5 mL crumbled dried sage)	15 mL
½ lb	old cheddar cheese, cut into small cubes	250 g
½	medium red bell pepper, finely diced	½
2–3	green onions, thinly sliced	2–3
to taste	salt and freshly ground black pepper	to taste

Cook the pasta in a large pot of lightly salted boiling water until just tender, about 7 to 8 minutes. While it cooks, place the mayonnaise, sour cream, mustard and sage in a large bowl and whisk to combine. Drain the cooked macaroni well, cool in ice-cold water, drain well again and place in the bowl. Add the remaining ingredients and toss to combine with the mayonnaise. Cover and refrigerate until serving time. (Can be made up to a day in advance.)

SOUTHERN-STYLE BROWN RICE SALAD

preparation time · 25 minutes
cooking time · 30–40 minutes (to cook rice)
makes · 8 servings

Fiber-rich brown rice tossed with black beans, chili powder, lime juice, Tabasco and a colorful mix of fresh vegetables makes a nice side dish for grilled meats, poultry and fish. It's also a great salad to bring to a summer potluck.

ERIC'S OPTIONS

For a more aromatic salad, use fragrant jasmine or basmati brown rice. If you don't care for the nuttier taste and texture of brown rice, substitute an equal amount of white long-grain rice.

3 cups	cooked, chilled brown rice	750 mL
1	19 oz (540 mL) can black beans, drained, rinsed in cold water, and drained again	1
8	cherry tomatoes, quartered	8
½ cup	finely diced yellow bell pepper	125 mL
½ cup	grated carrot	125 mL
3	green onions, thinly sliced	3
¼ cup	chopped fresh cilantro	60 mL
¼ cup	fresh lime juice	60 mL
1 Tbsp	honey	15 mL
1 tsp	chili powder	5 mL
1 tsp	ground cumin	5 mL
to taste	salt and Tabasco sauce	to taste
3 Tbsp	olive oil	45 mL

Place all ingredients in a large bowl and gently toss to combine. Cover and refrigerate until serving time. (Can be made up to a day in advance.) Toss the salad again just before serving to reincorporate any liquid ingredients that have sunk to the bottom of the bowl.

DELUXE
POTATO SALAD

preparation time	·	10 minutes
cooking time	·	10 minutes
makes	·	8 servings

Asparagus, whole-grain Dijon mustard, wine vinegar and sour cream are just a few of the ingredients that make this potato salad deluxe. I like to serve it with just about anything cooked on the barbecue, such as steaks, ribs and salmon.

ERIC'S OPTIONS
To make a lower-calorie version of this salad, use light versions of mayonnaise and sour cream.

1½ lb	red-skinned potatoes, cubed	750 g
½ cup	mayonnaise	125 mL
2 Tbsp	sour cream	30 mL
2 Tbsp	white wine vinegar	30 mL
2 Tbsp	whole-grain Dijon mustard (see Note)	30 mL
6	blanched asparagus spears, thinly sliced (see Note)	6
1	small carrot, grated	1
3	large hard-boiled eggs, chopped	3
2	green onions, sliced	2
to taste	salt and freshly ground black pepper	to taste

Gently boil the potatoes until just tender, about 10 minutes. Drain well and cool to room temperature. Place the mayonnaise, sour cream, vinegar and mustard in a large bowl and mix to combine. Add the potatoes, asparagus, carrot, egg, green onion, salt and pepper and gently toss to combine. Cover and refrigerate the salad until needed. (Can be made up to a day in advance.)

NOTE
Coarser whole-grain Dijon mustard is sold alongside the smooth Dijon at most supermarkets. To blanch the asparagus, cook in boiling water for 1 minute; drain well and plunge into ice-cold water to quickly cool it, and drain again.

BRIE and SUMMER BERRY SALAD

preparation time · 20 minutes
cooking time · none
makes · 4 servings

I came up with this salad during an August long weekend. The sweet berries, creamy cheese and earthy greens are a delightful taste combination and make a cool, light lunch on a hot day. Serve it with slices of French bread.

ERIC'S OPTIONS

Instead of brie, use any creamy cheese, such as small cubes of Camembert or nuggets of soft goat cheese. Baby spinach can also substitute for the salad greens.

¼ cup	olive oil	60 mL
1½ Tbsp	raspberry vinegar	22.5 mL
½ tsp	Dijon mustard	2 mL
2 tsp	honey	10 mL
½ tsp	tarragon	2 mL
to taste	salt and freshly ground black pepper	to taste
8 cups	mixed baby salad greens	2 L
½ cup	fresh raspberries	125 mL
⅓ cup	fresh blueberries	75 mL
8	strawberries, hulled and sliced	8
6 oz	brie cheese, cut into small cubes	175 g
⅓ cup	halved pecans or walnuts	75 mL

Place the oil, vinegar, mustard, honey, tarragon, salt and pepper in a salad bowl and whisk to combine. Add the salad greens and toss to coat. Divide the salad greens among 4 plates. Artfully top with the berries, cheese and pecans or walnuts and serve.

CORN on the COB with CURRY LIME BUTTER

preparation time · 10 minutes
cooking time · 2–3 minutes
makes · 6 servings

The fine flavor of fresh-picked corn is heightened even more with this simple preparation of spicy, tangy butter.

ERIC'S OPTIONS
For another taste element, provide a dish of chopped fresh cilantro, which your diners can sprinkle on the corn after slathering it with the butter.

¾ cup	butter, softened	175 mL
1 tsp	curry powder, or to taste	5 mL
1 tsp	finely grated lime zest	5 mL
1 Tbsp	fresh lime juice	15 mL
6	cobs of corn, shucked	6

Place the butter, curry powder, grated lime zest and juice in a small bowl and mix well to combine. Transfer to a small serving dish, cover and refrigerate until needed. (The butter can be made a day in advance.)

When ready to serve, let the butter soften to room temperature. Bring a large pot of water to a boil. Add the corn, return to a boil, and boil 2 to 3 minutes. Place the corn on plates and serve the flavored buttered on the table so guests can help themselves.

BAKED CHILLED SALMON with CREAMY SUMMER HERB SAUCE

preparation time · 20 minutes
cooking time · 15–18 minutes
makes · 8 servings

If you're looking for a classy lunch or dinner entrée to serve at a summer celebration on a hot day, try this simple chilled dish. Serve it with some of the salads found in this chapter, such as Deluxe Potato Salad (page 94) and Green Bean Salad with Tahini Dressing (page 91).

ERIC'S OPTIONS
The salmon and sauce can be prepared, covered and refrigerated up to a day in advance.

SAUCE

½ cup	mayonnaise	125 mL
½ cup	sour cream	125 mL
2 Tbsp	fresh lemon juice	30 mL
2 tsp	horseradish	10 mL
to taste	salt and white pepper	to taste
pinches	cayenne pepper and granulated sugar	pinches
¼ cup	chopped or snipped fresh herbs, such as dill, parsley, basil and chives	60 mL

SALMON

8	6 oz (175 g) salmon fillets	8
¼ cup	olive oil	60 mL
3 Tbsp	fresh lemon juice	45 mL
to taste	salt and white pepper	to taste
8	lemon wedges	8
8	fresh herb sprigs	8

Continued on the next page . . .

To make the sauce, place the mayonnaise, sour cream, lemon juice, horseradish, salt, white pepper, cayenne and sugar in a bowl and whisk to combine. Stir in the herbs. Cover and refrigerate until needed.

For the salmon, preheat the oven to 375°F (190°C). Line a baking sheet with parchment paper. Place the salmon in a single layer on the baking sheet. Combine the oil and lemon juice in a small bowl. Drizzle the mixture over the fish; season with salt and pepper. Cover and bake for 15 to 18 minutes, or until just cooked through. Cool the salmon to room temperature. Wrap and refrigerate for at least 2 hours, until well chilled. Place a piece of salmon on each of 8 dinner plates. Spoon some herb sauce alongside the fish. Garnish with a lemon wedge and herb sprig and serve.

WHEN IS FISH COOKED?

Fish is cooked when the translucent flesh becomes opaque and it begins to flake or to slightly separate and pull part. With fattier fish, such as salmon, white deposits of fat seep out between the flakes. When touched, cooked fish should feel slightly firm. If it feels hard, that's a sign you've overcooked it; if it's soft and spongy, it's not cooked through.

PICNIC
CHICKEN

preparation time · 20 minutes
cooking time · 40–45 minutes
makes · 6 (2 piece) servings

Cornmeal, sage, honey and mustard give this baked chicken its flavorful crunchy coating. Chilled well overnight in the refrigerator and kept in a cooler, it's perfect picnic food.

ERIC'S OPTIONS
For a sweeter, crisper crust, replace the breadcrumbs and cornmeal with 1 cup (250 mL) cornflake crumbs.

¾ cup	breadcrumbs	175 mL
¼ cup	cornmeal	60 mL
1 tsp	ground sage	5 mL
½ tsp	salt	2 mL
½ tsp	freshly ground black pepper	2 mL
⅓ cup	mayonnaise	75 mL
2 tsp	Dijon mustard	10 mL
2 tsp	liquid honey	10 mL
6	chicken drumsticks	6
6	chicken thighs	6

Preheat the oven to 375°F (190°C). Line a baking sheet with parchment paper. Combine the breadcrumbs, cornmeal, sage, salt and pepper in a wide, shallow bowl. Combine the mayonnaise, mustard and honey in another bowl. Add the chicken and toss to coat each piece well. Coat each piece of chicken in the breadcrumb mixture, gently pressing it on to help it adhere, and transfer to the baking sheet. Bake for 40 to 45 minutes, or until cooked through. Cool the chicken to room temperature. Chill in the refrigerator for at least 4 hours or overnight, before packing into an ice-cold cooler to enjoy at your picnic.

GRILLED RIB STEAK with ROASTED CORN, GREEN BEAN and POTATO SALAD

preparation time · 20 minutes
cooking time · about 25 minutes
makes · 4 servings

Celebrate a summer holiday evening at the cottage with this dinner that sees a prime, juicy beef steak deliciously paired with an easy-to-make summer salad.

ERIC'S OPTIONS

Grill any tender steak, such as T-bone or strip loin. For added flavor, brush the steaks with your favorite barbecue sauce when almost done.

NOTE

To blanch the beans, cook in boiling water for 2 minutes. Drain well, and immediately plunge into ice-cold water to chill them; drain well again.

1 lb	small white or Yukon gold potatoes, cut into small wedges	500 g
2	cobs of corn, kernels removed	2
3 Tbsp	olive oil	45 mL
1 tsp	ground cumin	5 mL
1 tsp	chili powder	5 mL
½ lb	green beans, trimmed, halved and blanched (see Note)	250 g
2–3 Tbsp	fresh lime juice	30–45 mL
pinch	granulated sugar	pinch
to taste	salt and freshly ground black pepper	to taste
4	8 oz (250 g) beef rib grilling steaks	4

Boil the potatoes in lightly salted water until just tender. Drain well and place in a wide bowl to cool. Preheat your barbecue to medium-high. Line a baking pan with parchment paper. Place the corn kernels, oil, cumin and chili powder in a bowl and toss to coat. Spoon into the baking pan. Set the pan on the upper rack of the barbecue and roast 10 minutes, stirring occasionally, until the corn is tender and nicely caramelized. Spoon the roasted corn and its cooking oil over the potatoes. Add the green beans and sprinkle the lime juice, sugar, salt and pepper over the salad. Toss to combine the ingredients.

Season the steaks with salt and pepper. Lightly oil the grate of your grill. Grill the steaks to the desired degree of doneness. Serve the steaks on individual plates with a generous spoonful of salad alongside.

GRILLING THE PERFECT STEAK: IT'S ALL A MATTER OF TOUCH

If you like rare or medium-rare steaks, choose those that are at least 1 inch (2.5 cm) thick. At high heat, they can be nicely seared on the outside while the inside remains rare. If you like steaks well done, choose thinner cuts, as thicker ones take a long time to cook through and become dried out.

When it's time to grill the steak, let it warm at room temperature for 20 minutes or so, depending on how hot a day it is. Never put an ice-cold steak on the grill; it won't cook evenly, as the outside will char and shrivel before the middle even gets warm. Be sure your grill is properly preheated before setting on the meat. If it's not, the meat can stick and you won't get nice grill marks.

Steaks become firmer the longer they cook. To see how it is progressing, lightly press the steak in the center (without squeezing out the juice) using the tips of your tongs or, carefully, with your finger.

A rare steak will feel soft to the touch in the very center. Medium-rare ones will be somewhat soft, but offer a little resistance. A medium steak will start to feel firm but still have a little give in the middle. Well-done steaks will feel firm all over.

Determining doneness by touch takes practice. To judge how your skill is progressing, make a small incision into the thickest part of a steak to check its doneness. After you've practiced and perfected your steak cooking skills, you won't have to do this.

BURGER BUFFET

preparation time · 30 minutes
cooking time · about 8 minutes
makes · 8 burgers

Celebrate your country's birthday by having a backyard barbecue with your family and friends. Place the grilled burgers on a platter, provide a basketful of buns and arrange the condiments and toppings in bowls and on plates. Then relax and allow your guests to build their own perfect burgers.

ERIC'S OPTIONS

For a more complex taste, use a mix of ground beef, pork and veal to make the burgers. Or, make lamb burgers by using ground lamb instead of beef.

2½ lb	lean ground beef	1.25 kg
⅓ cup	breadcrumbs	75 mL
4	green onions, thinly sliced	4
1	large egg, beaten	1
1 Tbsp	Worcestershire sauce	15 mL
1 tsp	Tabasco sauce	5 mL
1 Tbsp	chopped fresh rosemary	15 mL
1 tsp	salt	5 mL
1 tsp	freshly ground black pepper	5 mL
8	crusty burger buns, warmed	8
	assorted burger toppings, such as shredded lettuce, sliced tomatoes, onion, hot peppers, pickles, crispy bacon, grated cheddar and mozzarella cheese, relish, mustard, ketchup, barbecue sauce, salsa and guacamole	

Place the beef, breadcrumbs, green onions, egg, Worcestershire, Tabasco, rosemary, salt and pepper in a large bowl and mix until just combined. Moisten your hands with cold water and shape the meat into 8 patties, each about ¾ inch (2 cm) thick, placing them in a single layer on a large platter. (These can be prepared several hours in advance; cover and refrigerate.)

Preheat your barbecue to medium-high. Grill the burgers for about 4 minutes per side, or until entirely cooked through and the center of each burger reaches 160°F (71°C) on an instant-read meat thermometer.

Place the burgers on a clean platter with the buns nearby, set out the toppings and serve.

SHAPING AND COOKING BEEF BURGERS

Thoroughly wash your hands before handling ground meat. When mixing and forming the burgers, use a gentle touch; if you overmix, the meat will compact and toughen when cooked. Moisten your hands with cold water before shaping the burgers to prevent the meat from sticking.

Don't make your patties too thin (they can quickly overcook and dry out) or too thick (the exterior can scorch before the middle is cooked); ¾ inch (2 cm) thick is ideal. It's thick enough to provide a juicy center and a nicely seared exterior, but thin enough that the burger cooks in a reasonable amount of time. Wash your hands and all implements thoroughly after shaping the burgers.

When cooking, don't push down on the burger; that will squeeze all the flavorful juices out. Cooked beef patties will be brown throughout, with juices that have no pinkish tones. To kill any potential disease-causing bacteria, ground beef must be cooked to 160°F (71°C) or above. The safest way to test ground beef for doneness is by horizontally inserting an instant-read digital meat thermometer (sold at stores selling kitchenware) into the center of the patty. When the burgers are cooked, place them on a clean plate, not the one they were on when raw.

PORK BACK RIBS with CHERRY BARBECUE SAUCE

preparation time	·	25 minutes
cooking time	·	1 hour 45 minutes
makes	·	6 (½ rack) servings

I'm a fan of all kinds of ribs, but when grilling, I prefer to use pork back ribs. They are cut from the loin and are much leaner than pork side (spare) ribs, which are cut from the belly. As a result, they're less prone to flaring when set over the fire. They also have a lot of meat in between each bone—and all that tasty meat melds beautifully with this tangy sauce.

ERIC'S OPTIONS
The ribs can be cooked in the oven, cooled to room temperature and refrigerated in the morning. Grill when needed, allowing a few more minutes of cooking time as you will be starting from cold.

3	whole racks pork back ribs, each cut in half	3
1¼ cups	apple juice	310 mL
to taste	salt and freshly ground black pepper	to taste
1 cup	stemmed and pitted fresh cherries (about 18 to 20)	250 mL
½ cup	barbecue sauce	125 mL
¼ cup	orange juice	60 mL
¼ cup	fresh lime juice	60 mL
¼ cup	pomegranate or red currant jelly	60 mL
¼ cup	molasses	60 mL
1 Tbsp	Dijon mustard	15 mL
2 Tbsp	rice vinegar	30 mL
⅛ tsp	cayenne pepper	0.5 mL
⅛ tsp	ground allspice	0.5 mL
2 tsp	cornstarch	10 mL
3 Tbsp	water	45 mL

Continued on page 106 . . .

Pictured with Corn on the Cob with Curry Lime Butter, page 96

PORK BACK RIBS with CHERRY BARBECUE SAUCE *(continued)*

Preheat the oven to 325°F (160°C). Set the ribs, meaty side up, in a single layer in a large roasting pan or baking pan with sides. Pour in the apple juice; season the ribs with salt and pepper. Cover and bake 90 minutes, or until tender.

While the ribs cook, make the sauce by combining the cherries, barbecue sauce, orange and lime juice, jelly, molasses, mustard, vinegar, cayenne and allspice in a medium-sized pot. Gently simmer over medium heat for 10 minutes. Purée the mixture in a blender or food processor, or in the pot with an immersion blender. Return the sauce to a simmer. Mix the cornstarch and water together in a small bowl and stir into the cherry mixture. Simmer until it's lightly thickened, about 2 minutes. Remove the sauce from the heat.

When the ribs are ready, remove from the oven and uncover them. Preheat the barbecue to medium heat. Grill the ribs for a few minutes on each side. Place the ribs meaty side up and brush on a thick coating of sauce. Cook the ribs a few minutes more to heat the sauce through. Serve any leftover sauce at the table for drizzling over the ribs.

SMOKY GLAZED
BARBECUED HAM

preparation time ·	10 minutes
cooking time ·	about 65 minutes
makes ·	12 servings

One summer, my wife and I had invited a crowd over for my birthday and I thought a prepared, bone-in ham, which is sold fully cooked and just needs to be heated through, would make a simple but grand main course. It was a hot day and to avoid heating the house up, I decided to use the barbecue instead.

ERIC'S OPTIONS
Instead of maple syrup, use honey in the glaze.

1 cup	mesquite, hickory or other wood chips	250 mL
6–7 lb	bone-in, shank portion ham	2.7–3.15 kg
1 cup	apple juice	250 mL
¼ cup	maple syrup	60 mL
3 Tbsp	Dijon mustard	45 mL

Soak the wood chips in cold water for 1 hour. Drain them and place in your smoker box, or seal inside an 18- × 12-inch (45 × 30 cm) piece of aluminum foil. If you're using foil, poke the packet several times with the tip of a paring knife.

Preheat the barbecue to medium-high. Trim the ham of any tough outer skin. Score the top of the ham in a diamond pattern, making shallow cuts about 1 inch (2.5 cm) apart. Set the ham, cut (flat) side down in a large cast iron skillet or roasting pan suitable for the barbecue, or in a large tin foil pan. Pour in the apple juice. Loosely cover the ham with foil and place it on one side of the barbecue. Turn the heat off underneath the ham; leave the other side of the barbecue set to medium-high. Close the lid and cook 40 minutes. Make the glaze by combining the syrup and mustard in a small bowl.

After the ham has cooked 40 minutes, remove the foil and brush with one-third of the glaze. Set the wood chips directly on the coals on the lit side of the barbecue. Close the lid and cook the ham, without the foil, for 10 minutes. Brush with one-third more of the glaze and cook 10 minutes more. Brush the ham with the remaining glaze and heat through for a few minutes. Remove from the heat, tent the ham with foil and let rest for 10 to 15 minutes before slicing.

LUSCIOUS LAYERED ICE CREAM CAKE

preparation time · 20 minutes, plus refreezing time
cooking time · none
makes · 12 servings

This cake is a sublime ending to a summer barbecue. It will really impress your guests because it looks amazing, but it's surprisingly easy to assemble. The recipe gives you options on what types of ice cream you can use, so you can literally make the cake to suit your taste.

ERIC'S OPTIONS
This cake can be prepared several days in advance of serving. I like to prepare this cake in the morning, when my house has not yet been warmed by hot summer weather.

1 cup	graham cracker crumbs	250 mL
¼ cup	butter, melted	60 mL
2 Tbsp	granulated sugar	30 mL
2 tsp	cocoa powder	10 mL
4 cups	vanilla or chocolate ice cream	1 L
4 cups	cherry or strawberry ice cream	1 L
2 oz	semisweet chocolate, coarsely chopped	60 g
2 Tbsp	whipping cream	30 mL
12	fresh cherries or strawberries	12

Cut a circle of parchment paper to fit the bottom of a 10-inch (3 L) springform cake pan. Combine the graham crackers, butter, sugar and cocoa powder in a bowl and mix well. Pack the mixture into the bottom of the pan. Place the pan in the freezer until the crust is set, about 20 minutes.

Allow the vanilla or chocolate ice cream to soften at room temperature, about 10 to 15 minutes, until it's soft enough to spread. Scoop the ice cream into the cake pan and use a spatula to spread and evenly pack it down over the crust. Put the cake back into the freezer until the ice cream is firm, about 30 minutes.

Meanwhile, allow the cherry or strawberry ice cream to soften at room temperature. Take the cake out of the freezer and spread another layer of ice cream over the first one. Place the cake back in the freezer until the ice cream is firm.

Place the chopped chocolate and whipping cream in a small bowl, and microwave in short spurts until the chocolate is melted, stirring after each heating. Stir until smooth and evenly combined with the cream. (You can also heat the chocolate and cream together in a bowl set over simmering water.)

Remove the cake from the freezer and drizzle the top of it with the chocolate mixture. Return to the freezer and keep frozen, wrapping it with plastic wrap once the chocolate has set.

To serve, run a paring knife dampened with hot water around the outer edge of the pan. Remove the outer ring. Cut the cake into wedges and place on dessert plates. Garnish each serving with a whole cherry or strawberry. Serve immediately.

OATMEAL COOKIES with MIXED FRUIT and PECANS

preparation time · 20 minutes
cooking time · 30 minutes (15 minutes per cookie sheet)
makes · 30 cookies

The oats, fruit and nuts in these cookies provide ample energy for tossing the Frisbee several hundred times or making countless dives into the lake.

ERIC'S OPTIONS
These cookies freeze well in a tightly sealed container. If time allows, make a double batch and freeze the extras. If you're taking them to a picnic, they should thaw by the time you're ready to serve them.

1 cup	butter, softened	250 mL
1 cup	packed golden brown sugar	250 mL
2	large eggs	2
1 tsp	pure vanilla extract	5 mL
1 tsp	ground cinnamon	5 mL
pinch	ground nutmeg and cloves	pinch
½ tsp	salt	2 mL
½ tsp	baking soda	2 mL
3 cups	quick-cooking oats	750 mL
1 cup	all-purpose flour	250 mL
½ cup	dried cranberries	125 mL
½ cup	golden raisins	125 mL
½ cup	pecan pieces	125 mL
¼ cup	currants	60 mL
¼ cup	unsweetened coconut flakes	60 mL

Preheat the oven to 350°F (180°C). Line two 13- × 18-inch (33 × 45 cm) baking sheets with parchment paper. Beat the butter and brown sugar in a bowl until well combined and lightened. Beat in the eggs. Mix in the vanilla, cinnamon, nutmeg, cloves, salt and baking soda. Add the oats, flour, cranberries, raisins, pecans, currants and coconut and mix until well combined. Roll the dough into 1½-inch (4 cm) balls and place on the baking sheets, spacing the cookies about 2 to 3 inches (5 to 8 cm) apart. Press the balls into ½-inch-thick (1 cm) disks. Bake the cookies, one sheet at a time, for 15 minutes, or until light golden and cooked through.

Pictured with Homemade Lemonade with Raspberries and Mint, page 79

LEMON BLUEBERRY TARTS

preparation time · 25 minutes
cooking time · 25 minutes
makes · 12 tarts

This old favorite, lemon tarts, is taken to new heights with the addition of sweet blueberries. If you enjoy making pastry, by all means use your own, but the tart shells available in the frozen foods aisle of most supermarkets are a boon to busy cooks.

ERIC'S OPTIONS
Instead of blueberries, top the tarts with fresh raspberries, blackberries or a mix of fresh berries.

12	3-inch (8 cm) frozen tart shells, thawed	12
3	large eggs	3
½ cup	fresh lemon juice	125 mL
½ cup	granulated sugar	125 mL
2 Tbsp	melted butter	30 mL
2 cups	fresh blueberries	500 mL
for dusting	icing sugar	for dusting

Preheat the oven to 375°F (190°C) and place a rack in the middle position. Place the tart shells on a parchment paper–lined baking sheet. Poke the bottom of each tart with a fork a few times to prevent the pastry from puffing as it bakes. Bake for 10 minutes. Remove from the oven and cool to room temperature. Leave the oven on.

Place the eggs in a medium bowl and beat until the whites and yolks are well blended. Mix in the lemon juice, granulated sugar and butter until well combined. Pour the mixture evenly into the tart shells, filling them as close to the top as possible. Return the tarts to the oven and bake for 15 minutes, or until the filling is set. Cool to room temperature and then chill in the refrigerator for at least an hour.

Carefully remove the foil liners and place the tarts on a platter. Top each tart with 9 to 12 blueberries, depending on their size. Cover and refrigerate until serving time. (Can be prepared several hours in advance.) Just before serving, lightly dust each tart with icing sugar.

MENUS

This picnic will serve 6—perhaps a few more if young children have only one piece of chicken each. Make a quick exit the day of the picnic by doing the food preparation the day before, something that can be done with all items. Preparing the food ahead of time also ensures the perishable foods will have thoroughly chilled in your refrigerator and remain that way in a cooler with ice packs. Be sure to pack some cold drinks and also check out Planning a Summer Picnic (page 83).

- Picnic Chicken (page 99)
- Green Bean Salad with Tahini Dressing (page 91)
- Mac and Cheese Salad (page 92)
- Oatmeal Cookies with Mixed Fruit and Pecans (page 110)

SNACKING AND SIPPING ON THE PATIO

If you enjoy hosting summer gatherings but don't want to have a plated, sit-down dinner, a snack menu is always a popular way to feed guests. Fill serving platters with an assortment of easy-to-make, snack-sized portions of food that use minimal ingredients but still look and taste great. If you serve the wide variety suggested in this menu, your feast of finger foods can substitute for dinner. All recipes in the menu include advance preparation tips. The menu will feed 8 people, providing about 9 appetizer-sized portions each. Double the sangria recipe if you want to serve more than one glass per person.

- Fruity Rosé Sangria (page 80)
- Roasted Red Pepper Hummus (page 84)
- Fig and Olive Tapenade (page 86)
- Shrimp with Pesto on Grilled Zucchini (page 87)
- Curried Lamb Skewers with Mint Yogurt (page 89)
- Cherry Tomato and Goat Cheese Bruschetta (page 90)

Continued on the next page . . .

BACKYARD FATHER'S DAY FEAST

Here's a dinner where Dad can cook the main entrée on the barbecue—perhaps that new one he got for Father's Day—while the family takes care of the rest of the meal. Serve the salsa as an appetizer with tortilla chips for dunking. Accompany the ham and salad with corn on the cob, crusty buns and, if Dad has a really big appetite, some baked potatoes. The ice cream cake can be prepared a few days in advance, waiting in the freezer for you to decide when it's time to devour it. The menu serves 8. If you're not serving that many, don't worry, you'll have tasty leftovers to enjoy.

- Homemade Lemonade with Raspberries and Mint (page 79)
- Technicolor Summer Salsa (page 82)
- Smoky Glazed Barbecued Ham (page 107)
- Southern-Style Brown Rice Salad (page 93)
- Luscious Layered Ice Cream Cake (page 108)

SUMMER LONG WEEKEND BARBECUE

Nothing says summer better than an extra day off and a fine meal to celebrate, such as something succulent cooked on the barbecue. All the recipes in this menu include advance preparation tips. The tender ribs are glazed with a sauce infused with the taste of fresh, in-season cherries. Potato salad and corn on the cob are the perfect side dishes for ribs, especially when you add some crusty rolls and ice-cold beer or a fruity summer drink. The tarts bring a sweet end to this relaxing summer meal. The menu will serve 6.

- Pork Back Ribs with Cherry Barbecue Sauce (page 104)
- Deluxe Potato Salad (page 94)
- Corn on the Cob with Curry Lime Butter (page 96)
- Lemon Blueberry Tarts (page 112)

FALL FEASTS

CHAPTER FIVE

ROASTED
TOMATO TART

preparation time · 40 minutes plus chilling time
cooking time · 1 hour
makes · 6–8 servings

In early September, farmers' markets in my part of the world begin to fill with a colorful array of tomatoes, picked when ripe and bursting with flavor. That flavor intensifies when roasted in this savory tart. Bake the tart an hour before serving—it will take that long to set and be ready for slicing.

ERIC'S OPTIONS
This tart can be made oven-ready several hours in advance and refrigerated until you're ready to bake it.

1 cup	all-purpose flour	250 mL
¼ tsp	salt	1 mL
½ cup	vegetable shortening	125 mL
2	egg yolks mixed with 2 Tbsp (30 mL) ice-cold water	2
for greasing	vegetable oil spray	for greasing
2 Tbsp	extra virgin olive oil, plus some for drizzling	30 mL
1	large onion, halved and thinly sliced	1
1 cup	grated Swiss, Gouda or other tangy cheese	250 mL
5–6	ripe medium tomatoes (choose a mix of at least 2 colors), cut into ½-inch (1 cm) wedges	5–6
¼ cup	niçoise olives, pitted (see Note)	60 mL
1 tsp	herbes de Provence	5 mL
to taste	coarse sea salt and freshly ground black pepper	to taste
for drizzling	extra virgin olive oil	for drizzling

Continued on page 118 . . .

To make the pastry, place the flour and salt in a bowl. With a pastry cutter, fork, or your fingertips, work the shortening into the flour until a pea-sized crumble forms. Add the egg yolk/water mixture and gently work it in until the dough sticks together when gently squeezed. With lightly floured hands, gather the dough into a ball and press into a thick disk. Wrap and refrigerate for 15 minutes.

Spray a 9-inch (23 cm) tart pan with a removable bottom lightly with vegetable oil spray. Place the dough on a lightly floured surface and roll out into a 12-inch (30 cm) circle. Carefully transfer the dough to the tart pan and gently press into the pan. (If the pastry cracks, simply press it back together again.) Fold over any pastry hanging over the pan to make double-thick sides. Go over the tart pan with a rolling pin to cut off the edges. Chill the tart crust in the refrigerator for 1 hour.

Meanwhile, heat the olive oil in a skillet set over medium heat. Add the onion and cook until quite tender, about 5 to 6 minutes. Remove from the heat and cool to room temperature.

When the tart crust has fully chilled, preheat the oven to 325°F (160°C). Spread the onions into the bottom of the crust. Top the onion with the cheese.

Fan the tomatoes in an overlapping layer on top of the cheese. Arrange the olives on top of the tomatoes; sprinkle the tart with herbes de Provence, salt and pepper. Bake the tart in the middle of the oven for 1 hour. Cool on a baking rack to room temperature. Carefully unmold the tart, cut into wedges and serve with extra virgin olive oil on the side so diners can drizzle the tart, if desired.

NOTE
Small black niçoise olives are available at most supermarkets and delicatessens.

CHANTERELLE MUSHROOM CROSTINI

30/1/10 – Supper Club @ Rush's good!

preparation time · 20 minutes
cooking time · 18 minutes
makes · 12 crostini

In many wooded parts of North America, autumn rains bring chanterelle mushrooms. They are harvested and find their way to fine food stores and some supermarkets. They have an attractive golden color and are trumpet-shaped, with an intriguing, earthy taste and a pleasing, slightly chewy texture. For more about chanterelles, see the next page.

ERIC'S OPTIONS
If chanterelles are unavailable, use another type of mushroom, such as brown or oyster mushrooms.

½ lb	fresh chanterelle mushrooms	250 g
2 Tbsp	olive oil	30 mL
1	garlic clove, minced	1
¼ cup	white wine	60 mL
1 tsp	chopped fresh rosemary	5 mL
to taste	salt and freshly ground black pepper	to taste
12	thin slices baguette	12
¼ lb	soft goat cheese	125 g
for drizzling	balsamic vinegar	for drizzling

Trim the tips of the mushroom stems. Clean each mushroom well and then slice them thinly lengthwise. Place the oil in a large skillet over medium-high heat. Add the mushrooms and garlic and cook until tender, about 5 minutes. Add the wine and rosemary and bring to a simmer. Simmer until the wine has almost entirely cooked away. Season with salt and pepper and remove from the heat.

Preheat the oven to 375°F (190°C). Line a baking sheet with parchment paper. Spread the baguette slices with the goat cheese and place on the baking sheet. Top each crostini with some mushrooms. Bake, in the middle of the oven, for 10 minutes, or until the crostini are hot and toasted on the bottom.

Cool the crostini for a few minutes before arranging on a platter. Serve the balsamic vinegar alongside so diners can drizzle the crostini with it.

ABOUT CHANTERELLE MUSHROOMS

Chanterelle mushrooms grow in wooded areas in many parts of North America. They are esteemed for their fruity aroma and pleasingly chewy texture. There is a similar species of this mushroom, the white chanterelle, which you don't often see for sale.

When purchasing chanterelles, look for evenly colored, firm caps with no dark, soft or slimy spots or cracking. If very fresh, they'll keep well in a paper bag in the refrigerator for several days. Clean chanterelles well before cooking, removing any loose debris or dirt with a small, fine brush or paper towel.

In the fall, you'll find fresh chanterelle mushrooms for sale at farmers' markets, specialty food stores and some supermarkets. They can be expensive, but even a modest amount can make a dish extra special.

Cost is one reason some people pick their own chanterelles. If you are thinking about joining that club, it's essential that you learn all you can about harvesting wild mushrooms before even considering it. Toxic mushrooms grow in the same areas chanterelles do. One of the best ways to learn about wild mushrooms is to join a local mycological group. Such groups will share valuable information and tips on all things related to fungi.

AUTUMN VEGETABLE SOUP with TOASTED HAZELNUTS

preparation time	·	30 minutes
cooking time	·	about 30 minutes
makes	·	6–8 servings

Squash and root vegetables come into their own in the fall, when shorter days and crisper nights make us crave hearty fare. This soup, warmed with ginger and topped with crunchy nuts, is just the thing.

ERIC'S OPTIONS
If you don't care for hazelnuts, substitute toasted, sliced almonds.

2 Tbsp	olive oil	30 mL
1	medium parsnip, peeled and chopped	1
1	medium carrot, peeled and chopped	1
½	medium onion, chopped	½
1½ cups	peeled and cubed banana or butternut squash	375 mL
1	garlic clove, chopped	1
1 Tbsp	chopped fresh ginger	15 mL
2 Tbsp	all-purpose flour	30 mL
4¼ cups	chicken or vegetable stock	1.06 L
½ tsp	dried thyme	2 mL
pinches	ground nutmeg and ground cloves	pinches
to taste	salt and white pepper	to taste
1 cup	whole, shelled hazelnuts, toasted, skin removed and coarsely crushed (see Note on next page)	250 mL

Heat the oil in a medium-sized pot over medium heat. Add the parsnip, carrot, onion, squash, garlic and ginger and cook until softened, about 5 minutes. Mix in the flour and cook 2 to 3 minutes more. Slowly, continuing to stir, mix in the stock. Add the thyme, nutmeg and cloves. Bring to a gentle simmer and cook until the vegetables are very tender, about 20 minutes. Purée the soup in a food processor or blender, or in the pot with an immersion blender.

Return the soup to a simmer, thinning with a bit more stock if too thick, and season with salt and pepper. Ladle the soup into heated bowls. Sprinkle each serving generously with hazelnuts and serve.

NOTE
To toast hazelnuts and remove the skins, place in a single layer in a baking pan. Bake in a 350°F (180°C) oven for 15 to 20 minutes, or until lightly toasted and the skins start to crack. Transfer to a container, wrap tightly with plastic wrap and let stand 5 minutes. (The trapped steam will cause the skins to pull away from the nuts.) Use your hands to rub as much of the skins off the hazelnuts as you can. Place the nuts in a thick plastic bag and pound with a kitchen hammer to coarsely crush them. 1 cup (250 mL) of hazelnuts weighs about 3½ oz (100 g).

PUMPKIN CARROT SOUP with SPICE-ROASTED PECANS

preparation time · 25 minutes
cooking time · 30 minutes
makes · 6 servings

This autumn-colored soup can be made up to a day in advance, cooled to room temperature and refrigerated until ready to reheat. The pecans can also be roasted a day in advance, cooled to room temperature and stored in a tightly sealed jar.

ERIC'S OPTIONS
Instead of mixing the cream right into the soup, give the soup a more decorative look by drizzling and swirling the cream on top of each serving before sprinkling with the roasted pecans and parsley.

PECANS

⅓ cup	pecan halves, coarsely chopped	75 mL
2 tsp	vegetable oil	10 mL
¼ tsp	sea salt	1 mL
¼ tsp	granulated sugar	1 mL
¼ tsp	ground cumin	1 mL
¼ tsp	chili powder	1 mL
pinch	cayenne pepper	pinch

Preheat the oven to 325°F (160°C). Line a small baking pan with parchment paper. Place the pecans, oil, salt, sugar, cumin, chili powder and cayenne in a small bowl and toss to combine. Spread the pecans in a single layer in the pan. Bake in the middle of the oven for 10 minutes, or until the pecans are fragrant and lightly toasted.

Continued on the next page . . .

SOUP

2 Tbsp	olive oil	30 mL
2	medium carrots, peeled and chopped	2
½	medium onion, sliced	½
2	garlic cloves, crushed	2
2 Tbsp	all-purpose flour	30 mL
4 cups	chicken or vegetable stock	1 L
1	14 oz (398 mL) can pumpkin	1
1 tsp	dried crumbled sage	5 mL
¼ tsp	ground cinnamon	1 mL
pinch	nutmeg	pinch
¼ cup	light (10%) cream	60 mL
to taste	salt and freshly ground black pepper	to taste
1 Tbsp	chopped fresh parsley	15 mL

Place the oil in a medium-sized pot over medium heat. Add the carrots, onion and garlic and cook until softened, about 4 to 5 minutes. Stir in the flour and cook 2 minutes more. Slowly pour in the stock, stirring steadily. Stir in the pumpkin, sage, cinnamon and nutmeg and bring to a simmer. Simmer the soup 15 minutes, or until the carrots are tender. Purée the soup in a food processor or blender, or in the pot with an immersion blender. Return the soup to a simmer. Stir in the cream; season with salt and pepper. To serve, ladle the soup into heated bowls and top with the pecans and parsley.

MIXED SALAD GREENS with ROASTED GARLIC CAESAR DRESSING

preparation time ·	20 minutes
cooking time ·	40 minutes
makes ·	6–8 servings

Roasting garlic gives it a deliciously mellow taste—it's hard to believe the cup of salad dressing in this recipe contains six whole cloves.

ERIC'S OPTIONS
The dressing can be made several days in advance and refrigerated in a tightly sealed jar. For a more classic Caesar salad, instead of salad greens, use 12 cups (3 L) chopped romaine lettuce and add about 1½ cups (375 mL) of croutons to this salad after tossing with the dressing.

6	medium garlic cloves, peeled	6
1½ Tbsp	extra virgin olive oil	22.5 mL
¾ cup	mayonnaise	175 mL
2	anchovies, minced	2
1 Tbsp	fresh lemon juice	15 mL
2 tsp	Dijon mustard	10 mL
2 tsp	red wine vinegar	10 mL
¼ tsp	Worcestershire sauce	1 mL
¼ tsp	Tabasco	1 mL
to taste	freshly ground black pepper	to taste
12 cups	mixed baby salad greens	3 L
to taste	freshly grated Parmesan cheese	to taste

Preheat the oven to 300°F (150°C). Place the peeled garlic and olive oil in a small baking dish. Cover and roast 40 minutes, or until the garlic is very tender. Transfer the garlic and the oil in the dish to a small bowl. Smash the garlic with the back of a spoon until it has a pastelike consistency. Whisk in the mayonnaise, anchovies, lemon juice, mustard, vinegar, Worcestershire, Tabasco and pepper.

Place the salad greens in a large salad bowl. Toss in enough salad dressing to tastily coat the greens. (You may not need it all; refrigerate any leftover dressing for another salad.) Sprinkle the salad with Parmesan cheese and serve.

BAKED SALMON with MUSHROOM–PINOT NOIR SAUCE

preparation time · 20 minutes
cooking time · about 25 minutes
makes · 8 servings

Salmon is one fish that pairs well with red wine, particularly Pinot Noir. The recipe calls for only half a cup, and the remainder of the bottle, plus a few others, makes a fine accompaniment to the meal.

ERIC'S OPTIONS
The sauce could be readied up to a day in advance, then covered and stored in the fridge. To make the sauce a little more interesting, replace half the white or brown mushrooms with ¼ lb (125 g) oyster mushrooms (sliced) and ¼ lb (125 g) shiitake mushrooms (stems removed and discarded, and caps sliced).

8	5 oz (150 g) salmon fillets	8
4 Tbsp	olive oil	60 mL
to taste	salt and freshly ground black pepper	to taste
1 lb	white or brown mushrooms, sliced	500 g
2	medium shallots, finely chopped	2
1	garlic clove, minced	1
½ cup	Pinot Noir	125 mL
1 tsp	dried tarragon	1 mL
2 cups	whipping cream	500 mL
2 Tbsp	whole-grain Dijon mustard	30 mL
to taste	salt and freshly ground black pepper	to taste

Preheat the oven to 375°F (190°C). Place the salmon on a parchment paper–lined baking sheet. Brush with 2 Tbsp (30 mL) of the olive oil; season with salt and pepper. Bake for 15 to 18 minutes, or until cooked (see When Is Fish Cooked? on page 98).

While the salmon bakes, place the remaining 2 Tbsp (30 mL) olive oil in a large skillet and set over medium to medium-high heat. Add the mushrooms, shallots and garlic and cook until the mushrooms are tender, about 5 minutes. Add the wine and tarragon, bring to a simmer, and reduce to about 2 Tbsp (30 mL).

Add the whipping cream and mustard, return to a simmer and cook until it forms a lightly thickened sauce; season with salt and pepper. Place the salmon on individual serving plates, topped with the sauce.

SAUERBRATEN

preparation time	·	30 minutes, plus 2 days marinating time
cooking time	·	about 2 hours 45 minutes
makes	·	6–8 servings

Sauerbraten, when translated into English, means "sour roast." Red wine vinegar provides the sour taste in this braised beef dish. It has an unusual ingredient for a savory dish: gingersnap cookies (in the sauce). They add spice, and a sweetness that balances the sharp taste of the vinegar.

ERIC'S OPTIONS
If you have them on hand, for another taste of spice, add 8 to 10 juniper berries to the marinade mixture.

1½ cups	red wine	375 mL
½ cup	red wine vinegar	125 mL
2 cups	water	500 mL
1	medium onion, halved and thinly sliced	1
2	bay leaves	2
6	whole cloves	6
2 tsp	very coarsely ground black pepper	10 mL
1 tsp	salt	5 mL
4 lb	bottom round beef roast	2 kg
3 Tbsp	vegetable oil	45 mL
1	medium onion, diced	1
1	medium carrot, diced	1
2	medium celery ribs, peeled and diced	2
3 Tbsp	all-purpose flour	45 mL
½ cup	finely crushed gingersnaps (see Note next page)	125 mL

Place the wine, vinegar, water, sliced onion, bay leaves, cloves, pepper and salt in a pot and bring to a boil. Remove from the heat and cool to room temperature. Place the meat in a deep bowl and pour the wine mixture over the top. Cover, refrigerate and marinate for 2 days, turning the meat 2 to 3 times each day.

Continued on the next page . . .

Remove the meat from the marinade, place it on a plate and thoroughly pat it dry with paper towels. Strain the marinade through a fine sieve into another bowl.

Preheat the oven to 325°F (160°C). Place the oil in a Dutch oven or deep roasting pan over medium-high heat. Brown the beef on all sides; remove to a plate. Add the diced onion, carrot and celery to the pan and cook 3 to 4 minutes. Stir in the flour and cook 2 to 3 minutes more. Very slowly pour in the strained marinade while stirring, and bring to a simmer. Set the beef in the simmering sauce. Cover and cook in the oven 2½ hours, or until the meat is very tender.

Remove the meat to a plate, tent with foil and let it rest for 10 minutes. Skim the excess fat from the sauce. Place the pan on the stovetop and bring the sauce to a simmer. Add the gingersnaps and continue to simmer and stir until they are completely dissolved. Slice the meat and arrange on a platter. Drizzle with some of the sauce and serve the rest in a sauceboat alongside the meat.

NOTE

I crush my gingersnaps in a food processor. If you don't have one, place the cookies in a thick plastic bag and crush with a kitchen hammer or rolling pin.

POTATO PANCAKES

preparation time · 25 minutes
cooking time · 6–8 minutes
makes · 8 pancakes

This savory, crispy, German-style potato dish is irresistible—I like to serve it alongside slices of Sauerbraten (page 127). These pancakes could also be served with any pork roast, or if you'd like to eat them for breakfast, they make a nice base for a poached egg.

ERIC'S OPTIONS
The pancakes can be cooked in advance. Place on a large baking sheet lined with parchment paper, cool to room temperature, cover and refrigerate for up to a day. Reheat in a 300°F (150°C) oven for 10 to 15 minutes, or until heated through.

4	medium baking potatoes, peeled	4
2	large eggs, beaten	2
½ cup	finely grated onion	125 mL
2 Tbsp	flour	30 mL
½ tsp	salt	2 mL
¼ tsp	ground white pepper	1 mL
pinch	ground nutmeg	pinch
2 Tbsp	vegetable oil	30 mL

Preheat the oven to 200°F (95°C). Grate the potatoes, rinse well with cold water and drain in a colander. Thoroughly pat the potatoes dry with paper towels and place in a bowl. Mix in the egg, onion, flour, salt, white pepper and nutmeg. Coat the bottom of a large skillet or griddle with a thin layer of vegetable oil and warm over medium to medium-high heat. Working in batches (do not crowd the pan) and adding additional oil as needed, place dollops of the potato mixture in the pan using a ½ cup (125 mL) measure and spread them out to make 4- to 5-inch (10 to 12 cm) circles. Cook 3 to 4 minutes on each side, or until golden and crispy. Set the cooked pancakes on a heatproof platter and keep warm in the oven until all are cooked.

Pictured with Cranberry Pomegranate Sauce, page 137

ROAST TURKEY with
HERBES de PROVENCE and BUTTER

preparation time ·	20 minutes	
cooking time ·	about 2 hours 45 minutes–3 hours 15 minutes	
makes ·	8 servings	

Aromatic herbes de Provence is a French-style combination of herbs including thyme, rosemary, savory and lavender. Blended with butter and spread over the turkey before roasting, it gives the finished bird a wonderful flavor, aroma and appearance.

ERIC'S OPTIONS

Before roasting, stuff the bird with Whole Wheat Turkey Dressing with Apple and Bacon (page 136). Immediately before it goes in the oven, loosely fill the main cavity of the turkey and the cavity behind the large flap of skin at the neck end of the bird. Cook any remaining dressing in a pan as described in the dressing recipe. A stuffed turkey takes longer to cook; for this weight, you'll need to add 30 to 45 minutes more roasting time, or until the 180°F (82°C) temperature for a stuffed bird is achieved.

1	12–14 lb (5.5–6.3 kg) fresh or frozen (thawed) grade A or free-range turkey	1
3 Tbsp	butter, softened	45 mL
1 Tbsp	herbes de Provence	15 mL
to taste	salt and freshly ground black pepper	to taste
3½ cups	chicken or turkey stock	875 mL
⅓ cup	all-purpose flour	75 mL

Preheat the oven to 325°F (160°C). Place the turkey in a roasting pan. Remove the neck and innards from the cavity. Place the neck in the roasting pan and discard the innards unless you want—and know how—to use them. Tie the legs together with string; fold and tuck the wings under the body. Combine the butter and herbes de Provence in a small bowl. Brush the butter mixture over the surface of the turkey; season with salt and pepper. Roast the turkey uncovered for 1½ hours, and then give the roasting pan a 180-degree turn. Roast the turkey another 1 hour and 15 minutes.

Insert an instant-read meat thermometer deep into an inner thigh of the turkey, not touching the bone. If it reads 170°F (77°C), the turkey is ready. If not, baste the

Continued on the next page . . .

bird with the pan juices and roast 15 to 30 minutes more, or until the 170°F (77°C) temperature is achieved. Transfer the turkey and neck to a large platter, tent with foil and let it rest until you're ready to carve, at least 15 minutes.

To make the gravy, skim the fat from the pan drippings. Place the pan on the stovetop over medium-high heat. Add 3 cups (750 mL) of the stock to the pan and bring to a boil. Place the flour and the remaining ½ cup (125 mL) stock in a bowl and whisk until smooth. Whisk the mixture into the pan and simmer until the gravy thickens, about 5 minutes. Carve the turkey and serve the gravy in a sauceboat alongside.

A GUIDE TO PREPARING ROAST TURKEY

What size to buy

Many guides suggest allowing 1 lb (500 g) per person when buying turkey. If you're serving six people, however, it's unlikely you're going to find a 6 lb (2.7 kg) bird—tiny for a turkey. I recommend 1¼ to 1½ lb (625 to 750 g) per person, or even a little more if you want ample turkey leftovers from which to make sandwiches, soup and other dishes. Remember that the bigger the bird, the higher the meat-to-bone ratio tends to be, so it's safer to estimate less weight per person (1¼ lb/ 625 g) when buying a very large turkey, such as one that weighs over 20 lb (9 kg).

Storing and thawing

Buy fresh turkey a maximum of two to three days before you'll cook it and, if it's packed and sold at a supermarket, always check the best-before date. If buying a frozen bird, they tend to go on sale a few weeks before Thanksgiving and before Christmas, so buy it then and keep frozen until needed. Never thaw turkey on the kitchen counter at room temperature. The bird's exterior will thaw first and this may cause bacterial growth before the center of the turkey is thawed. The safest way is in the refrigerator. Allow 24 hours thawing time for every 5 lb (2.2 kg) of turkey, or even a bit more for very large birds. For example, a 12 to 14 lb (5.5 to 6.3 kg) turkey will take about three days to thaw.

To stuff or not to stuff

You can make dressing for turkey and bake it separately from the bird as described in Whole Wheat Turkey Dressing with Apple and Bacon (page 136). It will taste delicious and can be made oven-ready ahead of time, and you won't have to worry about the process of safely stuffing it inside the turkey.

However, many prefer to stuff the bird, as it can enhance the flavor of mild-tasting turkey and also produce a richer-tasting dressing. Always stuff the bird just before you put it in the oven. Fill the main cavity, making sure it's loosely stuffed, not packed in. If you pack it in, it won't get hot enough to kill any bacteria present in the turkey. Also stuff the cavity behind the large flap of skin at the neck end of the

Continued on the next page . . .

bird. You can pack the dressing tighter here as it's closer to the heat. Any leftover stuffing can be baked in a casserole dish.

Remove the stuffing from the turkey as soon as the bird is cooked. Transfer to a heatproof serving dish and keep warm in the oven while the turkey rests before carving. If the stuffing does not feel hot, bake until it reaches a bacteria-killing 165°F (74°C) when tested with an instant-read thermometer.

To baste or not to baste

Some folks put the turkey in the oven and don't open the door until it's done. Others occasionally baste it with the pan juices to keep the bird moist and give it a rich color. The more you open the oven door, however, the longer it will take for the turkey to cook.

I take an in-between approach. I let the turkey roast undisturbed until my first temperature check, which usually comes at a time when the bird is not quite cooked. Since I've opened the oven door to test the bird, it makes sense to baste it then as it will improve its color when it is fully cooked.

Cooking times

The charts on the facing page are for cooking a whole turkey without basting at an oven temperature of 325 to 350°F (160 to 180°C), using a regular (not a convection) oven. If you look at the whole turkeys for sale at your supermarket, you'll notice that even if they are the same weight, they will not all be uniform in shape. Some birds will have thicker breasts, others longer, thinner legs, all which can affect cooking time. That's why it is important to check for doneness about one hour before the end of the recommended roasting time. The turkey is done when an instant-read meat thermometer inserted deep into the inner thigh, not touching the bone, reads 170°F (77°C) for an unstuffed turkey or 180°F (82°C) for a stuffed one.

Roasting times for an unstuffed turkey			Roasting times for a stuffed turkey		
6–8 lb	(2.7–3.5 kg)	2½–2¾ hours	6–8 lb	(2.7–3.5 kg)	3–3½ hours
8–10 lb	(3.5–4.5 kg)	2¾–3 hours	8–10 lb	(3.5–4.5 kg)	3¼–3½ hours
10–12 lb	(4.5–5.5 kg)	3–3¼ hours	10–12 lb	(4.5–5.5 kg)	3½–3¾ hours
12–16 lb	(5.5–7.25 kg)	3¼–3½ hours	12–16 lb	(5.5–7.25 kg)	3¾–4 hours
16–20 lb	(7.25–9.0 kg)	3½–4½ hours	16–20 lb	(7.25–9.0 kg)	4–5 hours
20–25 lb	(9.0–11.25 kg)	4½–5 hours	20–25 lb	(9.0–11.25 kg)	5–6 hours

Carving the bird

After roasting, lift the turkey out of the pan and onto a large platter. Tent with foil and rest at least 15 minutes to set the juices (the turkey will stay hot a surprisingly long time). Use a sharp, thin-bladed carving knife to remove the leg and wing on one side of the turkey. Cut the leg into drumstick and thigh pieces; thinly slice meat from them. Carve the breast by making thin, slightly angled, vertical slices that run parallel to the breastbone. Repeat the process on the other side of the bird. Unless you're carving at the table, arrange the meat on a platter.

Handling leftovers

When the meal is done, remove any meat on the carcass as soon as you can. The cooked meat can be refrigerated for 2 to 3 days. You can also slice or dice the meat, put it in freezer bags or containers, and freeze for up to 2 months. To make turkey stock, break or cut the carcass into large chunks and place in a tall, large pot. Add a sliced onion, carrot, a celery stalk or two, a few whole black peppercorns, a pinch or two of dried thyme and 2 or 3 bay leaves. Add about 12 cups (3 L) of cold water, ensuring the bones are well covered. Gently simmer the stock (small bubbles should just break on the surface), uncovered, for 2 to 3 hours, or until a rich turkey taste is achieved. Add additional water during simmering, if necessary.

Strain the stock, cool and refrigerate. Remove any fat that has solidified on the surface. The stock is ready to use or be frozen for up to 2 months.

WHOLE WHEAT TURKEY
DRESSING with APPLE and BACON

preparation time · 25 minutes
cooking time · about 45 minutes
makes · 8 servings

This fiber-rich dressing is flavored with classic late autumn ingredients: sweet apples, smoky bacon and sage. Serve it with Roast Turkey with Herbes de Provence and Butter (page 131).

ERIC'S OPTIONS
The dressing can be made oven-ready several hours in advance. After spooning into the baking dish, cool to room temperature, then refrigerate. Pop the stuffing in the oven the moment the turkey is done.

10–12	slices whole wheat bread, cut into ½-inch (1 cm) cubes	10–12
4	strips bacon, diced	4
1	medium onion, finely chopped	1
2	celery ribs, finely chopped	2
1	large red apple, cored and cut into small cubes	1
1½ cups	chicken or turkey stock	375 mL
2 tsp	dried crumbled sage	10 mL
to taste	salt and freshly ground black pepper	to taste
2 Tbsp	butter, softened	30 mL

Place the bread cubes in a large bowl. Fry the bacon until crispy in a large skillet over medium to medium-high heat. Add the onion, celery and apple and cook 5 minutes more, or until tender. Spoon the mixture over the bread cubes. Add the stock, sage, salt and pepper and toss to combine.

Coat a 9- × 13-inch (3.5 L) baking dish with the butter. Spoon the dressing into the baking dish and cover with foil.

Preheat the oven to 375°F (190°C). Bake the dressing for 20 minutes. Uncover and bake 15 minutes more, or until the dressing is hot and crisp and golden on top.

CRANBERRY
POMEGRANATE SAUCE

preparation time	·	a few minutes
cooking time	·	20 minutes
makes	·	about 3 cups (750 mL)

Ruby-red, sweet and tangy, and aromatically spiced, this is a great condiment to serve alongside slices of roast turkey or any other poultry.

ERIC'S OPTIONS
If you really love the taste of ginger, replace the orange marmalade with ginger marmalade.

1 cup	orange marmalade	250 mL
¾ cup	pomegranate juice	175 mL
3 cups	fresh or frozen cranberries, about ⅔ lb (350 grams)	750 mL
¼ cup	packed golden brown sugar	60 mL
2 tsp	chopped fresh ginger	10 mL
½ tsp	ground cinnamon	2 mL
¼ tsp	ground cloves	1 mL

Place the marmalade and pomegranate juice in a medium-sized pot and bring to a simmer over medium to medium-high heat. Simmer and stir until the marmalade melts and blends with the juice, about 1 minute. Add the remaining ingredients, return to a simmer, and gently cook until the cranberries just begin to fall apart, about 15 minutes. Cool to room temperature, cover and refrigerate until needed. (Can be made up to a week in advance.)

BRUSSELS SPROUTS with GREMOLATA

preparation time · 20 minutes
cooking time · 4–5 minutes
makes · 6–8 servings

Gremolata is an Italian-style garnish made from a mix of chopped parsley, citrus zest and garlic. It's most often used to add a last minute, fresh taste to osso bucco (braised veal shanks). I discovered one day, having some gremolata leftover from making osso bucco, that it can also be a flavor-enhancing topping for a green vegetable, such as these Brussels sprouts. The gremolata ingredients can be chopped (together) a few hours in advance and refrigerated.

ERIC'S OPTIONS
Try the gremolata on other steamed or boiled green vegetables, such as asparagus, green beans or broccoli.

1 tsp	coarsely grated lemon zest	5 mL
1 tsp	coarsely grated orange zest	5 mL
8	parsley sprigs	8
1	garlic clove, thickly sliced	1
1½ lb	Brussels sprouts	750 g
2 Tbsp	melted butter	30 mL
to taste	salt and freshly ground black pepper	to taste

Bring a large pot of water to a boil. Place the lemon and orange zest, parsley and garlic together on a cutting board. Finely chop all the ingredients and place in a small bowl.

Boil the Brussels sprouts until just tender, about 4 to 5 minutes depending on size. (The Brussels sprouts used for this recipe were approximately 1 inch/ 2.5 cm in diameter. If yours are much larger, you'll need to boil them 1 to 2 minutes longer. See Cooking Brussels Sprouts on page 205.)

Drain well and place in a wide serving dish. Drizzle with the melted butter, season with salt and pepper, sprinkle with the gremolata and serve.

BRAISED RED CABBAGE with APPLES and WALNUTS

preparation time	·	15 minutes
cooking time	·	25–30 minutes
makes	·	6–8 servings

This nicely spiced cabbage, strewn with bits of apple and walnut pieces, goes very well with Sauerbraten (page 127) or any roast pork.

ERIC'S OPTIONS
Instead of apple, use 1 medium-sized pear, cored and cut into small cubes.

2 Tbsp	butter	30 mL
4 cups	cored and shredded red cabbage	1 L
1 cup	unsweetened apple juice	250 mL
2 Tbsp	apple cider vinegar	30 mL
½ tsp	ground cinnamon	2 mL
¼ tsp	ground cloves	1 mL
1	bay leaf	1
1	medium green apple, cored and cut into small cubes	1
⅓ cup	walnut pieces	75 mL
to taste	salt and freshly ground black pepper to taste	

Melt the butter in a pot over medium heat. Add the cabbage and cook until it softens, about 5 minutes. Add the apple juice, vinegar, cinnamon, clove, bay leaf, apple and walnuts and bring to a simmer. Cover, reduce the heat to medium-low, and cook 20 to 25 minutes, or until the cabbage is tender. Season the cabbage with salt and pepper and serve.

HONEY-GLAZED CARROTS with TOASTED ALMONDS

preparation time · 10 minutes
cooking time · about 15 minutes
makes · 8 servings

This easy-to-make carrot side dish is accented with sweet and sour flavors (honey and lemon) and crunchy textures (almonds).

ERIC'S OPTIONS
Instead of peeling and cutting whole carrots, use an equal weight of ready-to-use baby carrots in this recipe. Instead of honey, sweeten the carrots with maple syrup.

1½ lb	carrots, peeled	750 g
½ cup	sliced almonds	125 mL
2 Tbsp	butter	30 mL
2 Tbsp	liquid honey	30 mL
2 tsp	fresh lemon juice	10 mL
¼ cup	chicken or vegetable stock	60 mL
to taste	salt and freshly ground black pepper to taste	

Cut the carrots into 3-inch-long (8 cm), ¼-inch-wide (6 mm) sticks. Place in a pot, cover with cold water and boil until just tender, about 3 to 4 minutes. Drain well, cool in ice-cold water and drain well again. (Can be readied to this point a day in advance of serving. Place in a bowl and refrigerate until needed.)

Place the almonds in a thin layer in a large skillet over medium heat. Cook, swirling the pan from time to time, until lightly toasted, about 5 minutes. Remove from the heat and reserve.

Place the butter, honey, lemon juice and stock in a large skillet over medium to medium-high heat and bring to a simmer. Drain any water from the carrots and add them to the skillet. Cook, tossing them from time to time, until heated through, about 5 minutes. Season with salt and pepper, toss in the almonds and serve.

BAKED ACORN SQUASH with BROWN RICE and MUSHROOMS

preparation time	·	30 minutes
cooking time	·	about 65 minutes
makes	·	4 servings

Acorn squash, when it's halved lengthwise and the seeds are removed, makes an edible vessel that's perfect for stuffing and baking. In this case, the stuffing is a tasty mix of mushrooms, rice and vegetables that is a meal in itself.

ERIC'S OPTIONS
The squash can be readied up to a day in advance. After stuffing, cool the squash to room temperature, cover, refrigerate and bake when needed. Add 10 minutes or so to the baking time as they will be quite cold.

2	medium acorn squash	2
2 Tbsp	olive oil	30 mL
2	shallots, chopped	2
1	garlic clove, chopped	1
¼ lb	shiitake mushrooms, stems removed and discarded, caps sliced	125 g
¼ lb	oyster mushrooms, lower stems trimmed and discarded, top portion sliced	125 g
¼ lb	brown mushrooms, sliced	125 g
¼ cup	finely chopped red bell pepper	60 mL
¼ cup	grated carrots	60 mL
2	green onions, thinly sliced	2
1 Tbsp	chopped fresh sage	15 mL
2 cups	cooked brown rice, chilled	500 mL
⅓ cup	vegetable stock	75 mL
to taste	salt and freshly ground black pepper	to taste

Preheat the oven to 350°F (180°C). Cut each squash in half lengthwise. Scoop out the seeds and discard. Trim a little from the uncut side of each squash so it will sit flat. Place squash halves, cavity side down, on a parchment paper–lined baking sheet. Cover and bake for 35 to 45 minutes, or until the flesh just begins to soften.

Continued on the next page . . .

Meanwhile, prepare the filling by placing the olive oil in a large skillet over medium heat. Add the shallots, garlic, mushrooms, bell pepper and carrots and cook until the mushrooms are very tender, about 5 to 6 minutes. Place the mixture in a medium-sized bowl and mix in the green onions, sage, rice, stock, salt and pepper. Turn the squash halves, cavity side up, on the baking sheet and mound the mushroom mixture into them. Cover and bake 20 minutes, or until the squash is tender and the filling is heated through.

MAKE-AHEAD YUKON GOLD MASHED POTATO BAKE

preparation time · 15 minutes
cooking time · 40–45 minutes
makes · 8 servings

These mashed potatoes can be prepared up to a day in advance and baked when needed, eliminating that last-minute rush to mash potatoes when you're making a big meal—something every cook can use!

ERIC'S OPTIONS
Instead of the cheddar, use another flavorful cheese, such as Asiago or Swiss. For a tangy taste, use buttermilk instead of milk.

4 lb	Yukon gold (yellow-fleshed) potatoes, peeled and quartered	2 kg
1 cup	warm milk	250 mL
¼ cup	butter, melted, plus some for cassarole dish	60 mL
to taste	salt and white pepper	to taste
1½ cups	grated white cheddar cheese	375 mL
3	green onions, thinly sliced	3

Place the potatoes in a pot and cover with at least 2 inches (5 cm) of cold water. Bring to a boil and cook until the potatoes are very tender. Drain the potatoes well and mash thoroughly. Whip in the milk and melted butter. Season the potatoes with salt and pepper; mix in half of the cheese and two-thirds of the green onions. Lightly butter the bottom and sides of a shallow, 8-cup (2 L) casserole dish. Spread the potatoes in the casserole dish. Cool to room temperature, cover and refrigerate the potatoes and the remaining cheese and onion until needed.

Preheat the oven to 375°F (190°C). Sprinkle the potatoes with the remaining cheese and bake, uncovered, for 25 to 30 minutes, or until heated through and golden. Sprinkle with the remaining green onions and serve.

PHYLLO PEAR STRUDEL

preparation time	·	25 minutes
cooking time	·	25–30 minutes
makes	·	6–8 servings

Phyllo pastry is sold in the freezer section at most supermarkets; simply thaw and it's ready to use. In this recipe, phyllo gives the strudel a flaky, multilayered crust and bypasses the fussy, lengthy process of making traditional strudel dough.

ERIC'S OPTIONS
The strudel can be baked several hours in advance and served at room temperature. Dust with icing sugar just before serving. Instead of currants, soak and use an equal amount of raisins or dried cranberries.

⅓ cup	dried currants	75 mL
½ cup	hot water	125 mL
3	ripe medium pears, cored, quartered and thinly sliced	3
1 Tbsp	fresh lemon juice	15 mL
1 Tbsp	apple juice	15 mL
⅓ cup	packed golden brown sugar	75 mL
⅓ cup	pecan pieces	75 mL
1½ Tbsp	all-purpose flour	22.5 mL
½ tsp	ground cinnamon	2 mL
pinch	ground nutmeg and ground cloves	pinch
5	sheets phyllo pastry (see Handling Phyllo Pastry on facing page)	5
⅓ cup	melted butter	75 mL
1–2 Tbsp	icing sugar	15–30 mL
¾ cup	whipping cream, whipped	175 mL
6–8	mint sprigs for garnish (optional)	6–8

Place the currants in a small bowl and cover with the hot water. Let the currants plump up in the water for 30 minutes. Drain well and set aside.

Preheat the oven to 375°F (190°C). Line a large baking sheet with parchment. In a bowl, toss the pears with the lemon and apple juice. Add the soaked currants, brown sugar, pecans, flour, cinnamon, nutmeg and cloves; mix well to combine.

Place 1 sheet of the phyllo pastry on a large work surface and lightly brush with melted butter. Top it with another sheet of phyllo and brush it lightly with butter. Repeat until all 5 sheets are used.

Place the layered phyllo on the baking sheet and position the pan with the long side of the phyllo sheets facing you. Mound the pears along the bottom third of the pastry, leaving a 2-inch (5 cm) border along each side. Fold the sides of the pastry over the filling. Fold the bottom edge of the pastry up over the filling and carefully roll it up to completely enclose the filling. Center the strudel on the baking sheet. Brush the top of the pastry with butter. With a sharp serrated knife, make shallow, diagonal cuts, about 2 inches (5 cm) apart, on the top of the pastry to make it easier to cut after baking.

Bake for 25 to 30 minutes, or until puffed and golden. Allow the strudel to rest for 15 minutes before dusting with the icing sugar. Slice the strudel into portions with a sharp, serrated knife and set on plates. To serve, garnish each portion with a dollop of whipped cream and, if desired, a mint sprig.

HANDLING PHYLLO PASTRY

On a clear and large workspace, carefully unfold your package of phyllo pastry and remove the number of sheets you need. Cover those sheets with a slightly damp tea towel to prevent them from drying out. Carefully refold remaining phyllo, tightly seal and store in the refrigerator for up to 2 to 3 weeks, or refreeze for up to a month. For convenience, divide the phyllo sheets into several packages each containing the number of sheets you are most likely to use for your next recipe.

When brushing a sheet with butter or oil, ensure it gets a light and even coating before topping it with another. Be careful not to drench the sheets or the pastry will be soggy and limp, not light and flaky, once it's baked. When layering the sheets, don't be overly concerned if they aren't perfectly aligned or flat. The more you fuss the greater chance the sheets will tear or dry out.

ELIZABETH'S CRANBERRY BREAD

preparation time · 20 minutes
cooking time · 70–80 minutes
makes · 1 large loaf

This moist and delicious loaf with tangy, citrus flavors was a favorite in the household of Elizabeth Lawrence, a fine chef and friend of mine who passed away a few years ago. She was happy to share the recipe with anyone who loved this combination of flavors—including me!

ERIC'S OPTIONS
This recipe freezes well; double it and freeze one loaf for another time.

NOTE
The cranberries can be coarsely chopped with a sharp knife on a large cutting board, or pulsed in a food processor in batches.

2 cups	all-purpose flour	500 mL
1 cup	granulated sugar	250 mL
1½ tsp	baking powder	7 mL
½ tsp	baking soda	2 mL
1 tsp	salt	5 mL
¼ cup	butter, softened	60 mL
1	large egg, beaten	1
1 tsp	grated orange zest	5 mL
¾ cup	orange juice	175 mL
1½ cups	fresh or frozen cranberries, coarsely chopped (see Note)	375 mL
1½ cups	golden raisins	375 mL

Preheat the oven to 350°F (180°C). Grease a 9- × 5-inch loaf (2 L) pan with vegetable oil spray. Line the bottom of the pan with parchment paper. Sift the flour, sugar, baking powder, baking soda and salt into a large bowl. Cut in the butter until the mixture is crumbly. Add the egg, orange zest and orange juice all at once; stir just until the mixture is evenly moist. Fold in the cranberries and raisins. Spoon the batter into the prepared pan.

Bake for 70 to 80 minutes, or until the loaf springs back when gently touched in the very center with the tip of your finger. Cool in the pan for 5 minutes, then remove the loaf and cool on a baking rack. Cut the loaf into slices about ½ inch (1 cm) thick, and arrange on a decorative plate to serve.

FRESH
PUMPKIN PIE

preparation time · 60 minutes
cooking time · about 2 hours 55 minutes
makes · 2 pies; 16 servings

Pie pumpkins are smaller than the type of pumpkin you would carve for Halloween. They're about the size of a volleyball, but if you closed your eyes and picked one up you would guess it was much larger because of its weight. The dense, sweet flesh is great for cooking, puréeing and making superb pie. Pie pumpkins are sold at roadside farm stands, farmers' markets and some supermarkets.

ERIC'S OPTIONS

Make the pie crusts and the filling a day before you bake the pies. Cover and refrigerate separately. Give the filling a stir again before pouring into the shells and baking the pies.

If time is short, these pies can also be made with an equal amount of canned pumpkin.

PURÉE

| 1 | 5½ lb (2.5 kg) pie pumpkin | 1 |

CRUSTS

dough for 2 single pie crusts
(see Flaky Pie Dough on page 152)

FILLING

4	large eggs	4
3½ cups	fresh pumpkin purée	875 mL
1½ cups	evaporated milk	375 mL
1½ cups	packed golden brown sugar	375 mL
1 tsp	ground cinnamon	5 mL
¼ tsp	ground nutmeg	1 mL
pinch	ground cloves	pinch
½ tsp	salt	2 mL
1 cup	whipping cream, whipped	250 mL
for garnish	mint sprigs and pecan halves (optional)	for garnish

To make the purée, preheat the oven to 325°F (160°C). On a secured cutting board, trim off the stem of the pumpkin, and then cut the pumpkin into quarters. Use a paring knife to cut away most of the seeds and stringy bits and remove the rest with a large spoon.

Place the pumpkin in a large roasting pan, skin side down. Pour in cold water to a depth of 1 inch (2.5 cm). Tightly cover and bake the pumpkin 1¾ to 2 hours, or until the flesh is very tender. Uncover and cool to room temperature.

Remove the peel and purée the pumpkin flesh in a food processor. Spoon into a mixing bowl, cover and refrigerate until ready to make the filling.

To make the crusts, unwrap one of the disks of dough and place on a lightly floured work surface. Flour a rolling pin and roll the dough from the center out into a round large enough to fit a 10-inch (25 cm) wide pie plate with a 4 cup (1 L) capacity. Don't push too firmly; let the roller do the work. Turn the dough an eighth of a turn after each roll; this will help create a round shape and at the same time you can make sure the dough is not sticking. Sprinkle additional flour on the rolling pin and under the dough as necessary. When the round of dough is ready, carefully fold it in half and lay it across the center of the pie plate. Carefully unfold it and gently nestle it into the bottom of the plate. Crimp the top edges of the pie to create a finished look and trim off any excess dough from the side of the plate. Repeat with the other disk of dough. Refrigerate until the filling is ready.

When you are ready to prepare the filling, preheat the oven to 425°F (220°C). Beat the eggs in a large bowl until the yolks and whites are well blended. Whisk in the pumpkin, evaporated milk, brown sugar, cinnamon, nutmeg, cloves and salt. Pour the pumpkin mixture into the pie crusts. Bake for 15 minutes. Reduce the oven temperature to 350°F (180°C) and bake for 40 minutes more, or until the pie filling still jiggles slightly in the very center. Cool the pies on a baking rack to room temperature. Serve slices of the pie with a dollop of whipped cream and garnish with a mint sprig and pecan half.

FLAKY
PIE DOUGH

preparation time	·	10 minutes
cooking time	·	none
makes	·	dough for 1 double-crust pie or 2 single-crust pies

The generous amount of shortening (and a touch of butter) makes for an ultra-flaky crust.

ERIC'S OPTIONS
The dough, if tightly wrapped and kept refrigerated, could be prepared up to 2 days in advance. This dough also freezes well, so if you make a lot of pies, consider making a double batch and freezing the unused dough for another time. If tightly wrapped, the dough will keep up to 2 months in the freezer.

3 cups	all-purpose flour	750 mL
½ tsp	salt	2 mL
1¼ cups	cold vegetable shortening, cut into ½-inch (1 cm) cubes	310 mL
¼ cup	cold butter, cut into ½-inch (1 cm) cubes	60 mL
1	large egg, beaten with ⅓ cup (75 mL) ice-cold water	1

Combine the flour and salt in a bowl. With a pastry cutter or 2 forks (or with the paddle attachment of your stand mixer), cut the shortening and butter into the flour until well blended. Pour the egg/water mixture into the bowl; gently work it until it forms a loose, moist dough that just holds together. Transfer the dough to a lightly floured work surface. With lightly floured hands, shape the dough into a ball. Cut the ball in half. Press each half into a ½-inch-thick (1 cm) disk. Wrap and refrigerate each disk for 20 minutes before rolling out. If you've refrigerated the dough for more than 20 minutes and the fat in it becomes very firm, let the dough warm at room temperature for a few minutes before rolling it out.

MENUS

LABOR DAY WEEKEND FARMERS'S MARKET LUNCH

Farmers' markets seem at their peak on Labor Day, when local produce, such as radishes and lettuce, is still available and later crops, such as corn, root vegetables and tomatoes, are abundant. With such a fine selection, it's certainly a good time to celebrate the harvest by buying a basketful of produce and turning them into a wonderful, fall-is-almost-here lunch such as this one, which serves 6. All recipes include advance preparation tips.

- Autumn Vegetable Soup with Toasted Hazelnuts (page 121)
- Roasted Tomato Tart (page 116)
- Mixed Salad Greens with Roasted Garlic Caesar Dressing (page 125)
- Phyllo Pear Strudel (page 146)

THANKSGIVING DINNER

When preparing a Thanksgiving turkey dinner, it can be a struggle to have all the dishes ready at the same time. If that's you, it's understandable that you might start to get agitated even thinking about preparing the meal. This menu, which serves 8, maybe 10 if kids are at the table, was designed to relieve that anxiety. All the dishes except the turkey can be partially or entirely readied in advance (see recipes for details). This eliminates a lot of last-minute, stress-building racing around the kitchen. Read A Guide to Preparing Roast Turkey (page 133) before purchasing and cooking the bird.

- Roast Turkey with Herbes de Provence and Butter (page 131)
- Whole Wheat Turkey Dressing with Apple and Bacon (page 136)
- Brussels Sprouts with Gremolata (page 139)
- Make-Ahead Yukon Gold Mashed Potato Bake (page 145)
- Honey-Glazed Carrots with Toasted Almonds (page 141)
- Cranberry Pomegranate Sauce (page 137)
- Fresh Pumpkin Pie (page 150)

Continued on the next page . . .

VEGETARIAN THANKSGIVING DINNER

This tasty, seasonally inspired menu proves that you don't have to use meat to create a fine Thanksgiving dinner. The crostini, soup and squash recipes all serve 4, but could be expanded if you're serving a larger group. The cranberry bread is quite large and will serve at least 8. Any leftovers will taste great with tea the next day. Accompany the stuffed squash with a simple green salad. The soup and squash can be made ahead and reheated when needed.

- Chanterelle Mushroom Crostini (page 119)
- Pumpkin Carrot Soup with Spice-Roasted Pecans (page 123)
- Baked Acorn Squash with Brown Rice and Mushrooms (page 142)
- Elizabeth's Cranberry Bread (page 148)

OKTOBERFEST FEAST

A friend with German roots talked my wife and me into going to an Oktoberfest dinner/dance held annually in Victoria, BC. We had so much fun we now attend every year. At the event, several German-style, mixed plates of foods were offered and one contained sauerbraten, a sweet and sour slow-cooked beef dish, along with braised red cabbage and potato pancakes. It was so delicious I decided to try and create the meal at home and ended the dinner with strudel, a German-style dessert. It was a great success! This menu will serve 6 to 8. Play some German *oom-pah-pah* music, pour everyone a German beer and make plenty of toasts: *Prost!*

- Sauerbraten (page 127)
- Braised Red Cabbage with Apples and Walnuts (page 140)
- Potato Pancakes (page 129)
- Phyllo Pear Strudel (page 146)

HALLOWEEN TREATS

CHAPTER SIX

CRANBERRY MARTINIS with MELON EYEBALL SKEWERS

preparation time · 10 minutes
cooking time · none
makes · 4 drinks

Green melon balls, each studded with a dried cranberry, create the eerie, yet tasty, eyeball garnish used in this shimmering red cocktail. Use a melon baller, available at kitchenware stores, to scoop out the flesh of the melon.

ERIC'S OPTIONS
If you prefer, use ice-cold gin instead of vodka.

8	honeydew melon balls	8
4	dried cranberries	4
¾ cup	ice-cold regular or cranberry-flavored vodka	175 mL
¾ cup	cold cranberry juice	175 mL
1 tsp	ice-cold dry vermouth, or to taste	5 mL

Chill 4 martini glasses in the freezer. Use a paring knife to make a small slit in the center of each melon ball. Cut each cranberry in half widthwise, and push half a cranberry into each slit. Slide 2 melon balls on each of 4 cocktail picks or skewers.

Fill a cocktail shaker half full with ice. Pour in the vodka, cranberry juice and vermouth and shake until the shaker is too cold to handle. Strain the mixture into the chilled martini glasses. Garnish each martini with a melon skewer and serve immediately.

VAMPIRE
MARTINIS

preparation time · 10 minutes
cooking time · none
makes · 4 drinks

A cool cocktail, with a blood-red color that a vampire would love to sip on after a busy night. Each drink is ghoulishly garnished with a gummi worm.

ERIC'S OPTIONS
If you prefer, use ice-cold gin instead of vodka.

¾ cup	ice-cold vodka	175 mL
¼ cup	ice-cold Chambord or other raspberry-flavored liqueur	60 mL
1 cup	pomegranate juice	250 mL
4	gummi worm candies	4

Chill 4 martini glasses in the freezer. Fill a cocktail shaker half full with ice. Add the vodka, liqueur and pomegranate juice and shake until the cocktail shaker is too cold to handle. Strain into the chilled martini glasses. Decorate the rim of each glass with a gummi worm and serve.

MULLED
APPLE CIDER

preparation time · 10 minutes
cooking time · 30 minutes
makes · about 12 servings

This aromatic drink is perfect for a cool fall night, and it's designed for all ages.

ERIC'S OPTIONS
Instead of apple cider, use unsweetened apple juice.

1	small orange	1
2	cinnamon sticks, broken into pieces	2
2 tsp	whole allspice	10 mL
1 tsp	whole cloves	5 mL
12 cups	nonalcoholic apple cider	3 L
½ cup	liquid honey, or to taste	125 mL
¼ cup	fresh lemon juice, or to taste	60 mL
12	long cinnamon sticks (optional) for garnish	12

With a sharp paring knife, cut the peel (but not the pith) off the orange. Cut the peeled orange in half and squeeze the juice into a pot. Cut the orange peel into ½-inch (1 cm) slices. Place the orange peel, cinnamon sticks, allspice and cloves in a large tea ball or tie them up in a piece of cheesecloth and set in the pot. Add the cider, honey and lemon juice to the pot, bring to just below a simmer and heat on the stove for 30 minutes, or until nicely flavored with the spices and citrus flavors. Garnish each serving of mulled cider with a cinnamon stick, if desired.

TOMATO and ROASTED GARLIC CROSTINI

preparation time	·	30 minutes
cooking time	·	28–35 minutes
makes	·	24 crostini

Fresh-tasting bites with enough garlic to keep vampires away from your neck while you nibble.

ERIC'S OPTIONS
The tomato mixture and the toasted baguette slices could be made the morning before these crostini are served. Keep the tomato mixture refrigerated. The toasts can be covered and stored at room temperature until ready to top with the tomato mixture. If available, make these crostini more colorful by using a mix of different colored tomatoes, such as yellow, orange and red.

NOTE
To create bite-sized crostini, choose a baguette that is about 1½ inches (4 cm) in diameter.

6	medium garlic cloves, halved and very thinly sliced	6
4 Tbsp	olive oil	60 mL
24	¼-inch (6 mm) baguette slices (see Note)	24
4	medium vine-ripened tomatoes, seeds removed and flesh finely chopped	4
¼ cup	chopped fresh basil	60 mL
½	medium red onion, finely chopped	½
¼ cup	freshly grated Parmesan cheese	60 mL
to taste	salt and freshly ground black pepper	to taste

Preheat the oven to 300°F (150°C). Place the garlic and 2 Tbsp (30 mL) of the olive oil in a small baking dish. Cover with foil and roast the garlic 20 to 25 minutes, or until tender. Cool to room temperature.

Increase the oven temperature to 400°F (200°C). Place the baguette slices on a baking sheet. Brush the tops lightly with the remaining 2 Tbsp (30 mL) of olive oil. Bake until lightly toasted, about 8 to 10 minutes.

Place the tomatoes, basil, onion, cheese, salt, pepper and the roasted garlic and its oil in a bowl and mix to combine. Mound the tomato mixture on the baguette slices and serve immediately.

BLACK BEAN DIP in a PUMPKIN BOWL

preparation time	·	20 minutes
cooking time	·	none
makes	·	2 cups (500 mL)

This dip is similar to hummus but uses canned black beans instead of chickpeas. The black beans in the orange mini pumpkin bowls give this appetizer the two most common colors associated with Halloween. In the fall, mini pumpkins are available at most supermarkets and farm markets.

ERIC'S OPTIONS
If you don't care for the taste of cilantro, mix 3 thinly sliced green onions into the dip after processing instead.

1	mini pumpkin	1
1	19 oz (540 mL) can black beans, drained well, rinsed, and drained well again	1
2	garlic cloves, coarsely chopped	2
3 Tbsp	tahini	45 mL
¼ cup	olive oil	60 mL
¼ cup	fresh lemon juice	60 mL
1 tsp	ground cumin	5 mL
¼ tsp	chili powder	1 mL
¼ cup	chopped fresh cilantro	60 mL
to taste	salt and freshly ground black pepper	to taste

Cut the top of the pumpkin off as you would for a jack-o'-lantern. Scoop out the flesh and seeds from the pumpkin, creating a bowl for the dip.

Place the remaining ingredients in a food processor or blender. Pulse until smooth and well combined. Add a drop or two more of oil or water if you find the dip is too thick. Fill the hollowed-out pumpkin with the black bean dip. If the dip does not all fit, refrigerate the rest and refill the pumpkin when needed. (Can be made several hours in advance. Cover and refrigerate the dip-filled pumpkin until needed.) Place the pumpkin bowl on a tray and surround with crisp raw vegetable sticks and warm wedges of pita bread or Baked Tortilla Spikes (page 164) for dipping.

WEB-TOPPED
MEXICAN-STYLE LAYERED DIP

preparation time · 30 minutes
cooking time · none
makes · 10 servings

This popular dip is gussied up for Halloween with a spiderweb design. Serve it with Baked Tortilla Spikes (page 164) for dipping.

ERIC'S OPTIONS
Tailor the dip to your heat preference by choosing mild, medium or hot salsa.

1½ cups	shredded cheddar cheese	375 mL
⅓ cup	finely chopped red bell pepper	75 mL
3	green onions, thinly sliced	3
2	8 oz (250 g) bricks cream cheese, softened	2
1 cup	bottled tomato salsa	250 mL
1	ripe, medium avocado, peeled and cut into chunks	1
¼ cup	fresh lime juice	60 mL
½ tsp	granulated sugar	2 mL
¾ cup	sour cream	175 mL

Spread 1 cup (250 mL) of the shredded cheese into the bottom of a shallow-sided dish, such as a glass pie plate, about 9 or 10 inches (23 or 25 cm) wide. Sprinkle the red pepper and green onions overtop.

Place the cream cheese and salsa in a food processor; blend until it's almost smooth, but with a few pieces of the salsa still visible. Spoon the cream cheese mixture evenly into the serving dish, carefully spreading it out to the sides of the dish with a spatula.

Place the avocado, lime juice, sugar and ½ cup (125 mL) of the sour cream in a food processor and pulse until smooth. Carefully spread the avocado mixture over the cream cheese/salsa mixture, leaving a ½-inch (1 cm) border around the outer edge of the dish.

Place the remaining ¼ cup (50 mL) sour cream in a small piping bag fitted with a small, plain tip. Pipe a 1-inch-diameter (2.5 cm) ring of sour cream in the center of the dip. Pipe another ring about ½ inch (1 cm) out from the first one. Continue until the dip is topped with rings of sour cream. To create a weblike design, drag the tip of a paring knife from the center ring to the edge of the dip. Wipe the knife clean and repeat at 1-inch (2.5 cm) intervals around the dish, until the dip looks like it is topped with a spiderweb. Sprinkle the outer edges of the dip with the remaining ½ cup (125 mL) cheese. (Can be made several hours in advance. Keep refrigerated until needed. If you cover the dip with plastic wrap, don't allow it to touch the surface of the dip, or you'll mess up your spiderweb design.)

BAKED
TORTILLA SPIKES

preparation time · 10 minutes
cooking time · 10 minutes per baking sheet
makes · about 5 dozen spikes

Jagged, crisply baked tortillas perfect for dipping.

ERIC'S OPTIONS
Make these spikes more fiber-rich by using whole wheat tortillas.

⅓ cup	olive oil	75 mL
2 tsp	chili powder	10 mL
1 tsp	ground cumin	5 mL
4	10-inch (25 cm) flour tortilla shells	4
to taste	coarse sea salt	to taste

Preheat the oven to 350°F (180°C). Line 2 baking sheets with parchment paper. Combine the oil, chili powder and cumin in a small bowl. Cut the tortillas into 1-inch-wide (2.5 cm) strips. Cut the longer strips, cut from the center of the tortillas, widthwise in half at a slight angle. Brush the strips lightly with the oil mixture and arrange in a single layer on the baking sheets. Sprinkle the tortillas with salt. Bake, one sheet at a time, for 10 minutes, or until crisp and golden. Cool to room temperature. Store the spikes in a tightly sealed container until needed. The spikes can be made a day or two in advance.

STAKED STEAK with
RED-EYE DIPPING SAUCE

preparation time · 30 minutes plus marinating time
cooking time · 10–12 minutes
makes · 20 skewers

Tender steak is threaded on a skewer and roasted and served as an appetizer with the tangy sauce. A spoonful of ketchup or steak sauce dropped into the center of the sauce creates the red eye.

ERIC'S OPTIONS
Instead of beef, make these skewers with another type of tender meat, such as pork tenderloin or lamb sirloin. Once skewered, the meat can be refrigerated for several hours, until ready to roast.

3 Tbsp	olive oil	45 mL
1 Tbsp	balsamic vinegar	15 mL
2 tsp	chili powder	10 mL
1 tsp	ground cumin	5 mL
½ tsp	freshly ground black pepper	2 mL
2	garlic cloves, minced	2
1½ lb	strip loin or sirloin steak	750 g
to taste	salt	to taste
1½ cups	barbecue sauce	375 mL
½ cup	beef stock	125 mL
1	long, thick zucchini, cut in half lengthwise	1
¼ cup	ketchup or steak sauce	60 mL

Combine the oil, vinegar, chili powder, cumin, pepper and garlic in a medium-sized bowl. Cut the steak into 20 thin, long strips, place in the bowl and toss to coat. Cover and marinate in the refrigerator for 2 hours. Soak 20 wooden skewers in cold water for at least 1 hour.

Preheat the oven to 450°F (230°C). Line a baking sheet with parchment paper. Thread a slice of meat on one end of each skewer, leaving about 1½ inches (4 cm) of bare wood at the pointed end of each skewer. Place the skewers in a single layer on the baking sheet; season with salt.

Combine the barbecue sauce and stock in a small pot. Set the zucchini halves, cut side down, on a serving platter. Place a bowl for the dip on the platter.

Roast the skewers for 10 to 12 minutes, or a little longer if you prefer your meat well done. While the beef cooks, bring the sauce to a simmer over medium heat and simmer for 5 minutes.

When the beef is cooked, stand each skewer upright by sticking the pointed end of each skewer into the zucchini halves. Pour the sauce into the bowl. Create a red eye in the sauce by spooning the ketchup or steak sauce into the center of the bowl.

PUMPKIN CHILI with POBLANO PEPPERS and CORN

preparation time · 30 minutes
cooking time · 35 minutes
makes · 6–8 servings

You can dress up bowls of this vegetarian chili with a dollop of sour cream or yogurt, and add a sprinkling of shredded Monterey Jack cheese and sliced green onion or chopped cilantro.

ERIC'S OPTIONS
Dark green, fresh poblano peppers, which have a mildly spicy flavor, are available in the produce section of most supermarkets. If you can't find them, use 1 large green bell pepper in the chili and, if desired, add a splash or two of hot pepper sauce. To make squash chili, replace the pumpkin with cubes of butternut or banana squash. Cooking time and technique remains the same.

2 Tbsp	olive oil	30 mL
1	medium onion, diced	1
2	fresh poblano peppers, seeds removed and diced (see Eric's options)	2
1	large garlic clove, minced	1
4 cups	peeled, cubed fresh pumpkin	1 L
1	28 oz (796 mL) can diced tomatoes	1
2 cups	tomato sauce	500 mL
1 cup	beer or vegetable stock	250 mL
1	19 oz (540 mL) can black beans, drained and rinsed	1
1 cup	frozen corn kernels	250 mL
2 tsp	chili powder	10 mL
1 tsp	ground cumin	5 mL
1 tsp	dried oregano	5 mL
to taste	salt and freshly ground black pepper	to taste

Place the oil in a large pot over medium to medium-high heat. Add the onion, poblano peppers and garlic and cook 3 to 4 minutes. Add the remaining ingredients and bring to a gentle simmer. Reduce the heat and simmer, partially covered, for 30 minutes, or until the pumpkin is tender and the chili thickens. (Don't completely cover the chili when simmering. The steam must escape, not hit the top of the lid and fall back in the pot, which will cause the chili to be watery.)

Adjust the seasoning if necessary and serve.

CARVING PUMPKINS

It's impossible to celebrate Halloween without carving pumpkins. Here are some tips for making this illuminating occasion even more fun and tidier.

Buying the pumpkins
If you want your jack-o'-lanterns to have a distinctive look, purchase pumpkins that already have character—short and stout, tall and slim, lopsided or bumpy-skinned. These features give your pumpkin a personality even before you start carving it.

Plan ahead
Plan ahead and carve your pumpkins a day or two before Halloween. Keep them in a cool place, such as a garage or outdoor shed, until ready to light.

Have a pumpkin-carving party
Invite some family and friends, kids and adults, over to carve pumpkins. You can share ideas, have some laughs and marvel at how creative some folks can be.

Get organized and be safe
Pumpkin carving is fun, but it can be messy. Before you start, line a large work table with newspaper. Set out your tools for carving and scooping, a bowl of water to hold the seeds (see facing page), paper and pencils for creating designs and pens for drawing on the pumpkin. When the carving starts, an adult needs to be there to supervise and help kids when using carving tools.

Hollowing out the pumpkin
When cutting out the lid, angle the cut inwards to form a natural ledge for it to rest on. Hands are the best tools for removing the seeds, while a long metal spoon is best for scraping out the stringy bits on the inner walls. Use a paper towel to pat the outside of the pumpkin dry before drawing the design and carving.

Creating a design
If you're not a carving expert, first draw out your idea on a piece of paper. If you can't think of one, check the Internet for design ideas by entering "Halloween

pumpkin designs" in the search bar. Once you have a design you like, draw it on the pumpkin and then cut out the pieces to bring it to life.

Lighting up the pumpkin

Use short, votive-style candles secured in a heatproof dish or metal jar lid that rests evenly on the bottom of the pumpkin.

Roasting pumpkin seeds

Clean the seeds in cold water, removing any stringy bits. Pat dry, measure and place them in a bowl. For each 1 cup (250 mL) of seeds, mix in 1 Tbsp (15 mL) of vegetable oil and ¼ tsp (1 mL) salt, or to taste. If desired, add spices, such as Cajun spice or curry powder. Spread the seeds out in a single layer on baking sheets lined with parchment paper; roast at 350°F (180°C) for 15 to 20 minutes, or until nicely toasted.

MINI CHEESE BALL PUMPKINS

preparation time · 25 minutes
cooking time · none
makes · 24–30 pumpkins

I turned the mixture I used to make a regular cheddar cheese ball into these bite-sized mini cheese balls. When coated in crushed cracker crumbs and pushed down in the center, the squat shape is reminiscent of a pumpkin. Serve them as is, or set them on thin crackers. You can make these up to a day in advance.

ERIC'S OPTIONS
Instead of walnuts, use pecans.

NOTE
I use goldfish snack crackers for the coating, but any crisp, orange-colored cracker would work. I crush the crackers in a food processor; 1 cup (250 mL) yielded the perfect amount of crumbs.

1	8 oz (250 g) brick cream cheese, softened	1
1 cup	shredded cheddar cheese	250 mL
¼ cup	very finely chopped red onion	60 mL
¼ cup	walnut pieces, very finely chopped	60 mL
2 tsp	hot horseradish	10 mL
½ tsp	Worcestershire sauce	2 mL
¼ tsp	salt, or to taste	1 mL
½ cup	finely crushed orange colored crackers (see Note)	125 mL
24 pieces	green bell pepper, each ½ inch (1 cm) long and ⅛ inch (3 mm) wide	24 pieces

Line 2 baking sheets with parchment paper. Place the cream cheese in a bowl and beat with an electric mixer until lightened. Mix in the cheddar cheese, onion, walnuts, horseradish, Worcestershire and salt. Lightly dampen your hands with cold water. Shape the cheese mixture into ¾-inch (2 cm) balls and set on one of the baking sheets.

Place the cracker crumbs on a wide plate. Coat one of the cheese balls in the crumbs, gently pressing them on to help them adhere and shaping the ball so it has a nice round shape. Set it on the clean baking sheet. Repeat with the remaining cheese balls. Gently push down in the center of each cheese ball to give it a pumpkin shape. Make a stem by inserting a piece of green pepper into each cheese ball. Tent with plastic wrap and refrigerate at least 2 hours before serving.

HALLOWEEN
BROWNIE SQUARES

preparation time	·	30 minutes
cooking time	·	25 minutes
makes	·	24 bars

Here's a moist and delicious brownie that's given a Halloween look by spreading it with orange-colored icing and garnishing each square with a themed candy.

ERIC'S OPTIONS
Instead of walnuts, use pecan pieces in the brownies.

1 cup	butter, melted	250 mL
1 cup	granulated sugar	250 mL
¾ cup	packed golden brown sugar	175 mL
¾ cup	cocoa powder	175 mL
3	large eggs	3
1 cup	all-purpose flour	250 mL
1½ tsp	baking powder	7.5 mL
1½ tsp	pure vanilla extract	7.5 mL
1 cup	walnut pieces	250 mL
½ cup	cream cheese, softened	125 mL
¼ cup	butter, softened	60 mL
1½ cups	icing sugar	375 mL
	orange food coloring (see Note)	
24	Halloween-themed jellies or candies	24

Preheat the oven to 350°F (180°C). Grease a 9- × 13-inch (3.5 L) baking pan with vegetable oil spray. Cut a 13- × 13-inch (33 × 33 cm) piece of parchment paper to fit across the bottom and up 2 sides of the pan. (The parchment paper extending up the sides of the pan will be used as handles to lift the baked brownie out of the pan.)

Pour the melted butter into a large bowl. Beat in the granulated sugar, brown sugar and cocoa until well combined. Beat in the eggs, and then mix in the flour and baking powder. Stir in the vanilla and walnuts. Spoon the batter into the pan, spreading it evenly. Bake 25 minutes, or until the brownie springs back when gently touched in the center. Cool on a baking rack to room temperature.

Beat the cream cheese and the ¼ cup (60 mL) butter in a bowl until well combined and lightened. Beat in the icing sugar. Beat in drops of orange food coloring until the icing has a nice, Halloween-orange color.

Use a paring knife to loosen the brownie from the sides of the pan. Grab the parchment and lift the brownie out of the pan. Spread the icing over the brownie. Chill in the refrigerator for 1 hour to set the icing. Tent with plastic wrap until ready to serve. (The brownies can be made up to 2 days in advance of serving.)

Cut the brownie into 24 squares and set on a platter. Top each square with a Halloween candy. Keep the brownies refrigerated until you're ready to serve.

NOTE
Orange food coloring is available at stores that specialize in baking and decorating supplies. If you can't find it, add drops of red and yellow food coloring to the icing until you achieve an orange color.

DEVIL'S FOOD CUPCAKES

preparation time	·	35 minutes
cooking time	·	25 minutes
makes	·	24 cupcakes

Yummy, dense and chocolaty cupcakes—it won't be a surprise if you're a devil and eat two.

ERIC'S OPTIONS

These cupcakes freeze well. Set them in a single layer in a tightly sealed container and freeze for up to 2 months. Thaw at room temperature, ice them and garnish with the candy just before serving.

3 oz	unsweetened chocolate, chopped	90 g
1 tsp	baking soda	5 mL
½ cup	boiling water	125 mL
2 cups	butter, softened	500 mL
2 cups	granulated sugar	500 mL
5	large eggs	5
3 cups	all-purpose flour	750 mL
¾ cup	buttermilk	175 mL
1 tsp	pure vanilla extract	5 mL
2½ cups	icing sugar	625 mL
24	Halloween-themed candies	24

Preheat the oven to 350°F (180°C). Line 2 regular-sized, 12-cup (3 L) muffin tins with large paper baking cups. Melt the chocolate in a bowl over barely simmering water, and then remove from the heat. Dissolve the baking soda in the boiling water. Stir this mixture into the melted chocolate; set aside to cool slightly.

Place 1 cup (250 mL) of the butter and the granulated sugar in a large bowl and beat well to combine. Beat in the eggs one at a time. Continue beating until the mixture is thick and light yellow in color. Mix in the flour and buttermilk alternately. Mix in the melted chocolate mixture and the vanilla. Pour the batter into the paper cups. Bake 25 minutes, or until a cake tester comes out clean when inserted into the center of a cupcake. Cool the cupcakes in the muffin tins for 10 minutes. Remove the cupcakes from the tins and cool to room temperature on a rack.

Make the icing by beating the remaining 1 cup (250 mL) butter and icing sugar in a bowl until light and well combined. Spread or pipe the icing on the cupcakes. Decorate each cupcake with a Halloween candy. Keep cupcakes refrigerated until ready to serve. Cupcakes can be made up to a day in advance of serving.

PUMPKIN CHEESECAKE with MARZIPAN JACK-O'-LANTERNS

preparation time · 30 minutes
cooking time · about 85 minutes
makes · 12 servings

A moist, spice-filled cheesecake seasonally decorated with easy-to-make marzipan pumpkins. Marzipan is a paste made with ground almonds and sugar. It can be bought at some bakeries and supermarkets. Making the pumpkins takes some time and effort, but it's fun and can be a family activity.

ERIC'S OPTIONS

Cheesecake can be made up to 2 days in advance of serving. If making the marzipan pumpkins is too time consuming for you, omit and serve cheesecake portions with dollops of lightly sweetened whipped cream, garnished, if desired, with pecan halves.

PUMPKINS

½ lb	marzipan	250 g
	orange and black food coloring (see Note)	

CRUST

1¼ cups	finely crushed gingersnaps or graham cracker crumbs	310 mL
⅓ cup	melted butter	75 mL
¼ cup	granulated sugar	60 mL

FILLING

3	8 oz (250 g) bricks cream cheese, softened	3
1 cup	granulated sugar	250 mL
4	large eggs	4
1	14 oz (398 mL) can pumpkin	1
½ tsp	pure vanilla extract	2 mL
1 tsp	ground cinnamon	5 mL
¼ tsp	ground cloves	1 mL
¼ tsp	ground nutmeg	1 mL

Continued on the next page . . .

Set aside 3 Tbsp (45 mL) of the marzipan for decorating the pumpkins. Color the remaining marzipan orange by kneading drops of orange food coloring into it. Divide into 12 pieces and roll each into a ball. Gently press down on the balls to give them a squat, pumpkin shape. Use a wooden skewer or toothpick to mark in the ribs of the pumpkin.

Color the small piece of marzipan with black food coloring. Flatten it and cut or shape into handles, eyes, mouths and noses to decorate your marzipan pumpkins with. Set the pumpkins on a plate and cover and store at room temperature until needed. These can be made up to 2 days in advance.

To make the crust, combine the crust ingredients in a bowl and mix well. Press into the bottom and partially up the sides of a 10-inch (3 L) springform cake pan.

To make the filling, preheat the oven to 300°F (150°C). Place 1 rack in the lower third of the oven and another in the middle position. Beat the cream cheese in a bowl until smooth. Gradually beat in the sugar. Beat in the eggs one at a time, scraping the sides of the bowl after each addition. Mix in the pumpkin, vanilla, cinnamon, cloves and nutmeg. Pour the batter into the pan.

Place a shallow pan of water on the bottom rack of the oven; the steam rising from it will help prevent the cheesecake from cracking as it bakes. Set the cake on the rack above the water and bake 85 minutes, or until the center of the cake barely jiggles when the pan is tapped. Cool the cake on a baking rack for 15 minutes, and then run a sharp, thin and wet paring knife around the edges of the cake to a depth of 1 inch (2.5 cm). This will also prevent the cake from cracking as it cools and contracts. Cool the cake to room temperature. Cover and refrigerate in the pan for at least 3 hours.

When you're ready to serve the cake, run a wet paring knife completely around the outer edges of the pan to loosen the cake from the sides. Remove the cake pan's outer ring. Set the cheesecake on a cake plate. Arrange the pumpkins around the top edge of the cake. Slice and serve.

NOTE

Orange and black food coloring is available at stores that specialize in baking and decorating supplies. If you can't find them, use a mix of yellow and red food coloring, sold at most supermarkets, to create orange colored marzipan. Instead of black, simply use a color you do have, such as green.

PUMPKIN TARTS
FOR A PARTY

preparation time · 30 minutes
cooking time · 25 minutes per baking sheet of tarts
makes · 24 tarts

This recipe yields 24 tarts—a good number to bring to a Halloween potluck party for dessert. Because of the number of tarts you'll be baking, you'll need to cook them in two batches.

ERIC'S OPTIONS
Instead of nut halves and cranberry sauce, top each tart with a little whipped cream, dolloped on with a small spoon, or piped on with a piping bag fitted with a star tip.

24	3-inch (8 cm) tart shells	24
2	large eggs	2
1	14 oz (398 mL) can pumpkin purée	1
¾ cup	light (10%) cream	175 mL
¾ cup	packed golden brown sugar	175 mL
½ tsp	ground cinnamon	2 mL
¼ tsp	ground ginger	1 mL
pinch	ground cloves, nutmeg and salt	pinch
½ cup	cranberry sauce	125 mL
24	walnut or pecan halves	24

Place an oven rack in the middle position. Preheat the oven to 350°F (180°C). Line 2 baking sheets with parchment paper and place 12 tart shells on each sheet.

Beat the eggs lightly in a bowl. Whisk in the pumpkin, cream, brown sugar, cinnamon, ginger, cloves, nutmeg and salt. Fill 12 of the tart shells with half the filling. Bake for 25 minutes, or until the filling is set. Place on a rack to cool to room temperature.

When the first batch of tarts is done, fill the remaining 12 tart shells and bake them, then cool. When all the tarts have cooled to room temperature, refrigerate until needed. The tarts can be readied to this point up to a day in advance.

To serve, carefully remove the foil liners and arrange the tarts on a large platter. Set 1 tsp (5 mL) of the cranberry sauce in the center of each tart. Place a walnut half on the cranberry sauce and serve.

PLANNING A HALLOWEEN PARTY

If you're hosting a Halloween party and want some ideas on making it a lot of fun, consider these suggestions.

Ask your kids to decorate your front window with colored, Halloween-themed cutouts made from sturdy construction paper or other items they may have made at school. If you have them, string up Halloween-themed lights in the window.

If you would prefer not to dress up the house in cobwebs and other hard-to-clean-up stuff, try more simple accents. These could include Halloween-themed plates, serving trays, napkins and tablecloths; bowls of black and orange jelly beans or other candies; pumpkins; and ornamental gourds and corn.

Ask guests to bring a carved pumpkin to the party. Light them and arrange them in a good viewing place outside. Give guests a piece of paper and ask them to write down their favorite pumpkin. Count the ballots and give out a first, second and third prize.

Tell your guests, when inviting them, that at some point in the evening they will be voting on who has the best costume. This will encourage some of your guests to really go all out in getting dressed up. You could also give out prizes for the best costumes. If it's a big party, you can award prizes for best in category!

Play some suitably creepy music and spooky tunes during the party.

For kids, arrange to play a few games during the party, such as pin the tail on the cat (make a cat and some tails out of black construction paper) or pass the pumpkin (players sit in a circle and pass a small pumpkin until the music stops; the person with the pumpkin is out and the game continues until there is a winner).

MENUS

Halloween parties have become very popular, and for those interested in having a good time—whether young or old—it's easy to explain why. You dress up, act silly, laugh and have some food that's fun to eat. With this menu, which serves 8, you'll serve up a drink that's perfect for a cool autumn night, create a scary-looking spider web dip, make some spikes, cook a divine chili with in-season pumpkin, and be called devilish for making a dessert taste so good.

- Mulled Apple Cider (page 159)
- Web-Topped Mexican-Style Layered Dip (page 162)
- Baked Tortilla Spikes (page 164)
- Pumpkin Chili with Poblano Peppers and Corn (page 167)
- Devil's Food Cupcakes (page 174)

SIPPING AND SNACKING HALLOWEEN PARTY

This menu, featuring some frighteningly good martinis, is designed for an adult get-together, where guests get dressed up and party the night away with Halloween-themed drinks, appetizers and sweets. For an even more interesting mix of food and drink, ask your guests to bring an appetizer or drink—especially if you're having a large crowd over.

- Cranberry Martinis with Melon Eyeball Skewers (page 156) or Vampire Martinis (page 158)
- Tomato and Roasted Garlic Crostini (page 160)
- Black Bean Dip in a Pumpkin Bowl (page 161)
- Staked Steak with Red-Eye Dipping Sauce (page 165)
- Mini Cheese Ball Pumpkins (page 170)
- Halloween Brownie Squares (page 172)
- Pumpkin Tarts for a Party (page 180)

DECEMBER GATHERINGS

CHAPTER SEVEN

SMOKED SALMON TARTARE
on CUCUMBER ROUNDS

preparation time ·	30 minutes	
cooking time ·	none	
makes ·	20 pieces	

This is a significant spin on the classic dish beef tartare, where raw meat is chopped and mixed with tangy flavorings and displayed in pattylike form on a plate. In this version, finely chopped smoked salmon replaces the beef, and the tartare mixture is spooned on to palate-refreshing slices of cucumber, making a decadent appetizer.

ERIC'S OPTIONS
These bites can be made several hours in advance; cover and refrigerate until you're ready to serve. Instead of smoked salmon, use smoked tuna to make the tartare. You can find smoked tuna, which is usually frozen (thaw before using), at specialty seafood stores and some supermarkets.

¼ lb	smoked salmon, finely chopped	125 g
3 Tbsp	finely chopped red onion	45 mL
1 Tbsp	capers, finely chopped	15 mL
1 Tbsp	extra virgin olive oil	15 mL
2 tsp	fresh lemon juice	10 mL
1 tsp	Dijon mustard	5 mL
to taste	freshly ground black pepper	to taste
2 tsp	chopped fresh dill	10 mL
20	English cucumber slices cut ½ inch (1 cm) thick	20

Place the salmon, onion, capers, oil, lemon juice, mustard, pepper and dill in a bowl and gently mix to combine. Use a small spoon or melon baller to scoop out some of the center portion of each cucumber slice. Mound 2 tsp (10 mL) of the smoked salmon tartare in the center of each cucumber slice and arrange on a serving tray.

SHRIMP BISQUE
with CURRY

preparation time · 20 minutes
cooking time · 20 minutes
makes · 6 servings

Since seafood curries are popular in Southeast Asia, I wondered how the taste of curry powder would work in a French-style seafood soup. I gave it a try and the results were delicious. The curry gave the bisque an eye-appealing, golden hue, and the blend of spices used in that powder made the soup wonderfully aromatic and divinely flavored. This bisque will make a splendid start to any celebratory meal.

ERIC'S OPTIONS

This soup can be made up to a day in advance. After it's simmered 10 minutes and before the shrimp are added, cool to room temperature; cover and refrigerate. To serve, bring to a simmer and add the shrimp and garnish as described in the recipe instructions.

¼ cup	butter	60 mL
⅓ cup	finely chopped onion	75 mL
⅓ cup	finely chopped celery	75 mL
1	garlic clove, minced	1
¼ cup	all-purpose flour	60 mL
1 Tbsp	mild curry powder	15 mL
¼ tsp	paprika	1 mL
1½ Tbsp	tomato paste	22.5 mL
5 cups	chicken or fish stock	1.25 L
½ lb	small cooked salad shrimp, patted dry	250 g
¾ cup	light (10%) cream	175 mL
to taste	salt	to taste
3 oz	brandy (optional)	90 mL
2	green onions, thinly sliced	2

Melt the butter in a pot set over medium heat. Add the onion, celery and garlic and cook 3 to 4 minutes. Mix in the flour, curry powder, paprika and tomato paste and blend well.

Cook, stirring, 1 to 2 minutes more. While stirring, very slowly mix in the stock. Bring to a gentle simmer and simmer 10 minutes.

Set aside 30 of the shrimp to garnish the top of the soup. Mix the rest of the shrimp and the cream into the soup and heat through for 3 to 4 minutes. Season the soup with salt. Divide the brandy, if using, among 6 heated bowls. Ladle in the soup. Garnish the center of each serving with 5 shrimp and a sprinkle of green onion and serve.

TIPS FOR HOSTING LARGE DINNER PARTIES

When you're planning to host a dinner party for a large number of guests, the first thing to consider is what style of party it will be—a feast of appetizers, a buffet dinner or a more formal, sit-down meal. No matter what style you choose, select dishes that can be readied or partially readied in advance; you'll find dozens of such recipes in this book.

If you're having an appetizer or buffet dinner and seating is limited, some guests will be eating out of their laps or standing up. Choose foods that are friendly to this form of dining, such as small, bite-sized hors d'oeuvres and main-course dishes that can be eaten with a fork, no knife required.

When you're finalizing the menu, make sure all the dishes work within the budget you have set for the meal. Be firm about asking guests to RSVP. This will guide you in deciding how much food to prepare.

For easier cleanup, rent plates, glasses, cups, cutlery, a coffee pot, a punch bowl, tablecloths, napkins and any other items you may need from a rental company. It's less expensive than one might think and all you'll need to do before they go back is rinse the implements that held food or drink.

If you're serving wine and don't know what type or how much to buy, your best bet is to go to a well-run wine store with knowledgeable staff. They'll be able to make numerous suggestions in different price ranges and will be able to help you calculate how much wine to buy based on the number of people expected. If you do serve alcoholic beverages, make sure you have a plan for getting folks home if they overindulge.

TURKEY, VEGETABLE and BOW-TIE PASTA SOUP

preparation time · 20 minutes
cooking time · about 25 minutes
makes · 6 servings

If you have leftovers from a turkey dinner, this hearty soup is a delicious way to use it up. Served with slices of crusty Italian bread, it makes a nice lunch entrée.

ERIC'S OPTIONS
If you don't have turkey leftovers, buy a small piece of boneless, skinless turkey breast and roast, steam or fry it until cooked through; cut what you need for the soup. The soup could also be made with cooked, cubed chicken.

1 Tbsp	vegetable oil	15 mL
½	medium onion, diced	½
2	medium celery ribs, quartered lengthwise and thinly sliced	2
1	medium carrot, peeled and quartered lengthwise	1
2 Tbsp	tomato paste	30 mL
5 cups	turkey or chicken stock	1.25 L
1	14 oz (398 mL) can diced tomatoes	1
pinch	granulated sugar	pinch
1 cup	cooked turkey cut into small cubes	250 mL
1 cup	bow-tie or other bite-sized pasta	250 mL
2 Tbsp	store-bought or homemade pesto (see Pesto on page 88)	30 mL
to taste	salt and freshly ground black pepper to taste	

Heat the oil in a pot over medium heat. Add the onion, celery and carrot and cook 3 to 4 minutes. Mix in the tomato paste and cook 1 minute more. Add the stock, diced tomatoes, sugar and turkey, bring the soup to a simmer and simmer for 10 minutes. Add the pasta, return the soup to a simmer and cook until the pasta is tender, about 10 minutes. Stir in the pesto, season with salt and pepper and serve.

CREATING A CHEESE BOARD

One of the easiest and most impressive things to serve at a holiday party is a board of assorted quality cheeses. Here are some tips.

Types of cheese to serve
Provide an interesting mix of tastes by serving at least five different types of cheese. Offer different colors, shapes, textures and flavors, from meek and mild to bold and beautiful. Because there is such a vast variety of cheese available, it's a good idea to shop at a specialty store where the staff can offer suggestions and let you sample the cheeses.

But as a guide, try to include a firm cheese (such as aged Gouda-style cheese), a semisoft cheese (such as brie), a blue cheese (such as roquefort), a soft and creamy cheese (such as goat), and one that simply looks interesting (such as cheddar flavored with port). You could also include a homemade cheese log, such as Herbed Goat Cheese Logs (page 190).

How much to buy
When the cheese board is one of several appetizers, allow 2 to 3 oz (60 to 90 g) per person. When served as a snack or single appetizer with wine, or when served as a postdinner course, serve a more generous ¼ lb (125 g) per person.

How to serve
Unwrap the cheese and place on the cheese board 90 minutes before serving to allow it to warm to room temperature. Cover it loosely to allow the cheese to breathe (just like a good wine) but not dry out. Provide a different knife for each type of cheese, which helps avoid having the flavors intermingle. If you're serving a smaller group sitting around a table, present the cheese just as you buy them, and let guests help themselves. But if you'll be serving a larger, stand-up crowd, present some cheeses as described above, but cut some cheese in bite-sized pieces or cubes so guests can quickly sample some cheese and move out of the way to make room for others. Serve the cheese with good-quality crackers and/ or sliced baguette, nuts and dried and fresh fruit, such as walnuts, almonds, dried apricots, figs, apples and grapes.

HERBED
GOAT CHEESE LOGS

preparation time	·	20 minutes
cooking time	·	none
makes	·	2 logs; 12 to 16 servings

This Mediterranean-inspired appetizer is quick and easy. Set the cheese on a platter with a small serving knife or two, surround it with good crackers or thin slices of baguette, and invite your guests to help themselves. You could also include the log as part of a cheese board.

ERIC'S OPTIONS
Use green olives instead of black, or a mix of green and black olives. For a spicy taste, roll the logs in crushed black peppercorns instead of herbs. For a nutty taste, roll the logs in crushed walnuts.

¾ lb	soft goat cheese	375 g
3–4	canned artichoke hearts, very finely chopped	3–4
¼ cup	pitted black olives, very finely chopped	60 mL
8	oil-packed sun-dried tomatoes, drained well and very finely chopped	8
½–¾ cup	mixed chopped fresh herbs, such as parsley, basil and oregano	125–175 mL

Place the goat cheese in a bowl and beat until lightened and smooth. Mix in the artichokes, olives and sun-dried tomatoes. Lightly dampen your hands with cold water and divide the goat cheese mixture in half. Shape each half into a log that is 6 inches (15 cm) long and 2 inches (5 cm) in diameter.

Place the mixed herbs on a wide plate and stir until combined. Roll each log in the herbs, coating it well and gently pressing the herbs on to help them adhere. Wrap each log in plastic wrap and refrigerate for 2 hours to firm up. (The logs can be prepared up to a day in advance.)

See Creating a Cheese Board, page 189

MIXED SALAD GREENS with PEAR and POMEGRANATE

preparation time	·	20 minutes
cooking time	·	none
makes	·	6 servings

Start a festive dinner with this palate-awakening salad. It features a mix of light and refreshing tastes—tender greens, pears, orange juice, pomegranate seeds— that will stimulate your taste buds but won't fill you up, a good thing when more delicious food is to come.

ERIC'S OPTIONS
Instead of mixed baby salad greens, use baby spinach. For a less tart taste, substitute sweeter tasting balsamic vinegar for the red wine vinegar.

3 Tbsp	olive oil	45 mL
2 Tbsp	red wine vinegar	30 mL
2 Tbsp	orange juice	30 mL
¼ cup	walnut halves, finely chopped	60 mL
2 tsp	honey	10 mL
to taste	salt and freshly ground black pepper to taste	
10–12 cups	mixed baby salad greens	2.5–3 L
1	ripe medium pear, halved, cored and thinly sliced	1
⅓ cup	pomegranate seeds	75 mL

Place the oil, vinegar, orange juice, walnuts, honey, salt and pepper in a salad bowl. Mix well to combine. Add the salad greens and toss to coat. Divide the greens among 6 salad plates. Garnish the top of each salad with the pear slices and pomegranate seeds. Serve immediately.

HOW TO CLEAN A POMEGRANATE

If you need pomegranate seeds for a recipe, here is an efficient way of getting them out of the fruit fairly quickly.

Remove the crown at the top of the pomegranate almost like you would take the top off a pumpkin. Score the skin from top to bottom, cutting into the pomegranate about ⅛ inch (3 mm) deep; make 4 to 6 cuts depending on the size of the fruit.

Fill a bowl with cold water and submerge the pomegranate in it. Pull the pomegranate apart into sections that follow your score lines. Doing this underwater should prevent any juice from spurting on you.

Remove the seeds from the membranes; the seeds will sink to the bottom and the membranes should float to the surface. Discard the membranes.

Drain the seeds in a sieve. Dry on paper towel and they are ready to use.

WILD RICE SALAD with MIXED FRUIT and NUTS

preparation time	·	20 minutes
cooking time	·	25 minutes
makes	·	8 servings

You can make this fruit- and nut-rich salad up to a day in advance and keep it in the refrigerator. Toss again just before you serve it.

ERIC'S OPTIONS
If making this salad when mandarin oranges are unavailable, peel, remove the pith and dice 2 regular oranges and use them in the salad.

1¼ cups	wild rice (uncooked)	310 mL
½ cup	dried cranberries	125 mL
½ cup	golden raisins	125 mL
½ cup	currants	125 mL
½ cup	pecan pieces	125 mL
½ cup	unsalted roasted cashews	125 mL
3	mandarin oranges, peeled, separated into segments and sliced	3
3	green onions, thinly sliced	3
3 Tbsp	raspberry vinegar	45 mL
2 Tbsp	olive oil	30 mL
2 Tbsp	maple syrup or honey	30 mL
to taste	salt and freshly ground black pepper to taste	

Place the rice in a pot and add 5 cups (1.25 L) cold water. Bring to a boil over high heat. Lower the heat so that the water gently simmers. Simmer the rice until just tender, about 25 minutes. Drain well, cool to room temperature and place in a bowl. Toss in the remaining ingredients. Cover and refrigerate until you're ready to serve.

CRANBERRY MAPLE CHICKEN

preparation time · 25 minutes
cooking time · about 75 minutes
makes · 8 (2 piece) servings

This is a sumptuous dish created by braising chicken thighs and drumsticks with a fine mix and balance of flavors that include tangy cranberries, sweet maple syrup and rich, buttery pecans. It's pretty rich, so two pieces per person is an ample portion size. Serve the chicken with steamed rice and Broccoli Florets with

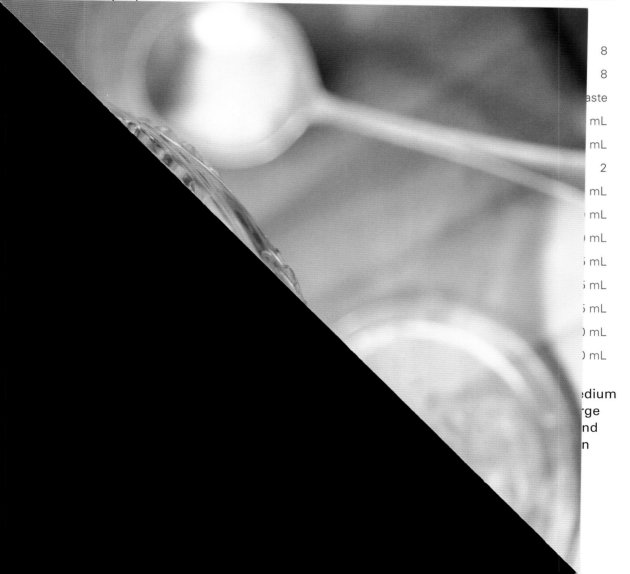

8

8

aste

mL

mL

2

mL

mL

mL

mL

mL

mL

mL

mL

edium

rge

nd

n

Heat the remaining 2 Tbsp (30 mL) of oil in a small pot over medium heat. Add the onion and cook 3 to 4 minutes. Add the ginger and cook 1 minute more. Add the maple syrup, stock, wine and vinegar, increase the heat to medium-high and bring to a boil. Divide and pour the mixture over the chicken. Sprinkle the chicken with the herbes de Provence. Nestle the cranberries and pecans around the chicken. Cover and bake for 60 minutes, or until the chicken is cooked and deliciously tender.

ROAST TURKEY BREAST with a TRIO of VEGETABLES and PAN GRAVY

preparation time ·	30 minutes	
cooking time ·	90 minutes	
makes ·	6–8 servings	

This recipe provides a simpler way to prepare roast turkey, vegetables and gravy for a festive dinner, such as Christmas. The vegetables are parboiled ahead of time and finished off in the roasting pan alongside the turkey. And while the turkey rests, the gravy is made in the same pan. Serve with mashed potatoes and Cranberry Pomegranate Sauce (page 137).

ERIC'S OPTIONS
The vegetables in this dish can be made oven-ready up to a day in advance, covered and refrigerated until needed.

¾ lb	baby carrots	375 g
2	large parsnips, peeled, halved lengthwise and sliced into ½-inch (1 cm) pieces	2
1½ lb	Brussels sprouts, trimmed	750 g
to taste	salt and freshly ground black pepper	to taste
5 Tbsp	olive oil or melted butter	75 mL
3 lb	boneless turkey breast roast	1.5 kg
2 tsp	crumbled dried sage	10 mL
¼ tsp	paprika	1 mL
3 cups	chicken or turkey stock mixed with ¼ cup (60 mL) all-purpose flour	750 mL

Place the carrots and parsnips in a pot and cover with cold water. Boil until firm/tender (tender on the outside, but still a little firm in the middle), about 4 to 5 minutes. Drain well, cool in ice-cold water, drain well again and place in a bowl. Cook the Brussels sprouts in rapidly boiling water until firm/tender, about 3 minutes. Drain well, cool in ice-cold water, drain well again and place in the bowl with the carrots and parsnips. Toss the vegetables with salt, pepper and 3 Tbsp (45 mL) of the oil or melted butter. Cover and refrigerate until you're ready to roast them.

Preheat the oven to 425°F (220°C). Place the turkey breast in a large roasting pan (you'll need the added room for the vegetables). Brush the turkey with the remaining 2 Tbsp (30 mL) of the oil or butter; sprinkle with the sage, paprika, salt and pepper and rub it over the turkey. Roast for 20 minutes. Reduce the heat to 325°F (160°C) and roast 25 minutes more. Surround the turkey with the prepared vegetables. Roast 45 minutes more, or until the center of the turkey reaches 170°F (77°C) on an instant-read meat thermometer and the vegetables are tender.

Remove the turkey from the pan and set on a plate. Tent with foil and rest 10 minutes. Spoon the vegetables into a serving dish, cover and keep warm in a 200°F (95°C) oven.

While the turkey rests, drain the excess fat from the roasting pan before placing on the stovetop over medium-high heat. Add the stock/flour mixture and bring to a simmer. Cook until thickened, about 5 minutes; season with salt and pepper. Slice the turkey and arrange it on a platter. Serve the gravy in a sauceboat and the vegetables alongside.

TURKEY TOURTIÈRE with YAMS and CRANBERRIES

preparation time ·	40 minutes	
cooking time ·	about 2 hours	
makes ·	6–8 servings	

This version of tourtière using ground turkey provides a tasty twist on the classic French Canadian meat pie usually made with pork. Serve, if desired, with your favorite chutneys and relishes—homemade if you have them.

ERIC'S OPTIONS
You can get the tourtière oven-ready a day in advance. Cover and refrigerate until ready to bake. It also freezes well unbaked. Thaw in the refrigerator overnight before baking as described.

1	medium yam	1
1¾ lb	ground turkey	875 g
½	medium onion, finely chopped	½
3 Tbsp	flour	45 mL
½ cup	chicken stock	125 mL
½ cup	dried cranberries	125 mL
1 tsp	dried crumbled sage	5 mL
½ tsp	ground cinnamon	2 mL
¼ tsp	ground cloves	1 mL
½ tsp	salt	2 mL
½ tsp	freshly ground black pepper	2 mL
pinch	ground nutmeg	pinch
2 Tbsp	chopped fresh parsley	30 mL
	dough for a double crust pie (see Flaky Pie Dough on page 152)	
1	large egg beaten with 2 Tbsp (30 mL) milk	1

Preheat the oven to 350°F (180°C). Prick the yam all over with a fork and place in a small baking pan. Bake until just tender, about 60 minutes. Cool the yam until it's safe to handle. Peel and cool to room temperature. Cut into small cubes and refrigerate until needed.

Place the turkey and onion in a pot over medium heat. Cook, stirring occasionally to break up the meat, until the turkey is cooked through. Mix in the flour until well incorporated. Slowly, stirring constantly, pour in the stock and cook 2 to 3 minutes more. Mix in the yam, cranberries, sage, cinnamon, cloves, salt, pepper, nutmeg and parsley. Remove from the heat and cool to room temperature. Cover and refrigerate until needed. (Filling can be made a day before you make the tourtière.)

Lightly flour your work surface and roll out one of the disks of dough into a circle that's ⅛ inch thick (3 mm) and 1½ inches (4 cm) larger than the top diameter of a 10-inch (25 cm) pie plate with a 4-cup (1 L) capacity. Fold the dough in half and lay it across the center of the pie plate. Carefully unfold it and gently nestle it into the bottom of the pie plate. Spoon the turkey mixture into the pie crust, gently packing it in.

Flour the work surface again, if necessary, and roll out the second disk of dough the same way. Fold it in half and lay it across the center of the pie plate. Carefully unfold it to cover the filling. Dust your fingers with flour and crimp the top and bottom crusts together. Trim away the excess crust with a paring knife. Brush the top of the tourtière with the beaten egg mixture. Cut a small hole in the very center of the tourtière to allow steam to escape as it bakes. Chill for 20 minutes in the refrigerator to firm up the pastry before baking.

Preheat the oven to 425°F (220°C). Bake the tourtière for 20 minutes. Reduce the heat to 350°F (180°C) and bake 30 minutes more. Allow the tourtière to set for 10 minutes before slicing.

ROAST CORNISH HENS GLAZED
with MAPLE and DIJON

preparation time · 25 minutes
cooking time · 50–55 minutes
makes · 8 servings

The glaze for these succulent hens is easy to make and hard to resist. It's a sweet, spicy and herbaceous mix of maple syrup, Dijon mustard and sage.

ERIC'S OPTIONS
Instead of maple syrup, use honey in the glaze for the hens. Instead of sage, flavor the hens with chopped fresh rosemary.

4	Cornish hens	4
to taste	salt and freshly ground black pepper	to taste
⅓ cup	maple syrup	75 mL
⅓ cup	Dijon mustard	75 mL
3 Tbsp	chopped fresh sage, or 2 tsp (10 mL) dried crumbled sage	45 mL

Preheat the oven to 375°F (190°C). Place 1 hen on a secure work surface and use kitchen shears or a sharp knife to cut along either side of the backbone and remove it. Place the hen breast side up and press it flat. Cut it in half down the middle of the breastbone. Place the hen halves, skin side up, in a large roasting pan. Repeat with the remaining hens. Season with salt and pepper. (The hens can be cut and made oven-ready several hours in advance of serving. Keep refrigerated until ready to roast.)

Roast for 30 minutes. Combine the maple syrup, mustard and sage in a bowl. Brush half the mixture over the hens and roast for 10 minutes. Brush with the remaining mixture and roast 10 to 15 minutes more, or until cooked through.

SAUTÉED BRUSSELS SPROUTS with GINGER, RED PEPPER and ORANGE

preparation time	·	15 minutes
cooking time	·	about 10 minutes
makes	·	8 servings

Enhanced with the flavor of butter, bell pepper, orange and ginger, these Brussels sprouts may even make their way on to the plates of those who are usually not that fond of them.

ERIC'S OPTIONS
For added texture and flavor, sprinkle the Brussels sprouts, once spooned into a serving dish, with ¼ to ⅓ cup (60 to 75 mL) toasted, sliced almonds.

1¾ lb	Brussels sprouts, trimmed	875 g
2 Tbsp	butter	30 mL
½	large red bell pepper, cut into small cubes	½
2 tsp	finely grated fresh ginger	10 mL
½ cup	orange juice	125 mL
to taste	salt and freshly ground black pepper to taste	

Bring a large pot of water to a rapid boil. Add the Brussels sprouts, return to a boil, and cook until just firm/tender, about 3 minutes, depending on the size. (The Brussels sprouts I used in this recipe were approximately 1 inch/2.5 cm in diameter. If yours are much larger, you'll need to boil them 1 to 2 minutes longer.) Drain well, cool in ice-cold water and drain well again. Place the sprouts in a bowl and refrigerate until needed. (They can be readied to this point up to a day before serving.)

To serve, melt the butter in a large skillet over medium heat. Add the bell pepper and ginger and cook 1 to 2 minutes. Drain off any water that's accumulated in the bottom of the bowl of Brussels sprouts; add the sprouts and the orange juice to the skillet. Increase the heat to medium-high and cook until the sprouts are heated through and the orange juice has started to thicken and form a glaze around them. Season with salt and pepper and serve.

COOKING BRUSSELS SPROUTS

When purchasing Brussels sprouts, choose vibrant green, firm sprouts that feel heavy for their size. Avoid yellowish sprouts with a lot of loose leaves—a sign they've been sitting around too long. To ensure even cooking, pick Brussels sprouts of roughly the same size. If you like a milder, somewhat sweeter taste, choose smaller ones, approximately 1 inch (2.5 cm) in diameter.

To prepare them for cooking, rinse the sprouts well in cold water, trim the stems and remove any loose outer leaves. Use a paring knife to cut a shallow cross into the bottom of the stem end of each Brussels sprout. This will allow the cooking liquid or steam to reach the center of the sprout and promote even cooking.

To cook, bring a large pot of water to a boil, then add the Brussels sprouts. Return to a boil, reduce the heat to a gentle boil and cook until the stem ends are just tender when pierced with a paring knife. This can take 4 to 8 minutes, depending on the size of the sprouts. If you prefer, steam the Brussels sprouts for a similar amount of time.

A good make-ahead technique, used in Sautéed Brussels Sprouts with Ginger, Red Pepper and Orange (page 204), is to blanch the sprouts in advance and them with the flavorings when ready to serve.

Brussels sprouts have a bad reputation among some people that pr from improper cooking and past-their-due-date vegetables. If ove bold-tasting vegetable can intensify in flavor and aroma and t grayish/green color. Properly cooked and seasoned, sprout winter table!

BROCCOLI FLORETS with ROASTED PEPPERS

Preparation time	·	20 minutes
Cooking time	·	15–20 minutes
Makes	·	8 servings

The green and red combination gives this side dish a Christmassy look.

ERIC'S OPTIONS
The broccoli can be made oven-ready several hours in advance. Cover and refrigerate until you're ready to bake it.

24	medium-sized broccoli florets	24
1	large roasted red pepper, finely chopped (see Note)	1
1 cup	chicken or vegetable stock	250 mL
½ tsp	dried oregano	2 mL
1	garlic clove, finely chopped	1
	ound black pepper to taste	

)oil. Add the broccoli
t 2 to 3 minutes. Drain
drain well again.
-inch (3.5 L) baking
epper, stock, oregano
mixture over the
t has some roasted
salt and pepper. Bake
a 325°F oven (160°C)
ed through.

jars at most
our own, see Eric's

eheat

obably stems
cooked, this
rn an unpalatable
can be a staple of the

SPICED
YAM ROUNDS

Preparation time	·	10 minutes
Cooking time	·	About 80 minutes
Makes	·	8 servings

This is an ultrasimple recipe, and I always get compliments when I serve it. You simply bake yams with the skin on, then cool, slice and set on a baking sheet. Baste them with this sweet, sour and spice-filled butter mixture, then bake. It's not rocket science!

ERIC'S OPTIONS
Instead of yams, bake, slice and use sweet potatoes in this dish.

3	small to medium yams (each about 3 inches/8 cm in diameter)	3
3 Tbsp	honey	45 mL
3 Tbsp	melted butter	45 mL
2 Tbsp	fresh lemon juice	30 mL
¼ tsp	ground cinnamon	1 mL
pinch	ground nutmeg, ginger and cloves	pinch
to taste	salt and freshly ground black pepper	to taste
1 Tbsp	chopped fresh parsley	15 mL

Preheat the oven to 325°F (160°C). Line a baking pan with parchment paper. Prick each yam several times with a fork and place in the pan. Bake until just tender, about 60 minutes. Cool the yams to room temperature. (The yams can be prepared to this point up to a day in advance. Cover and refrigerate until ready to slice and bake.)

Preheat the oven to 325°F (160°C). Line a baking sheet with parchment paper. Slice the yams into ½-inch-thick (1 cm) rounds and place on the baking sheet. Combine the honey, butter, lemon juice, cinnamon, nutmeg, ginger and cloves in a small bowl. Brush the mixture over the tops of the yams. Season with salt and pepper. Bake the yams, uncovered, for 20 minutes, or until heated through. Arrange on a platter, sprinkle with parsley and serve.

PECAN, COCONUT and CURRANT SQUARES

preparation time ·	20 minutes
cooking time ·	25 minutes
makes ·	36 squares

This dessert improves in flavor when the spices and other fine ingredients are allowed to mature for a few days after baking. Keep it tightly wrapped and refrigerated until you're ready to cut it into squares.

ERIC'S OPTIONS

The squares can be cut, placed in a tightly sealed container (place sheets of parchment paper between each layer if you stack them) and frozen for up to a month. Take out what you need and let them thaw at room temperature for 30 minutes before serving.

CRUST

½ cup	butter, softened	125 mL
½ cup	packed golden brown sugar	125 mL
1¼ cups	all-purpose flour	310 mL

FILLING

2	large eggs	2
½ cup	packed golden brown sugar	125 mL
½ cup	granulated sugar	125 mL
½ tsp	pure vanilla extract	2 mL
¼ tsp	ground cinnamon	1 mL
pinch	ground nutmeg and ground cloves	pinch
1 cup	pecan pieces	250 mL
⅓ cup	unsweetened medium coconut flakes	75 mL
⅓ cup	currants	75 mL

Cut a 9- × 13-inch (23 × 33 cm) piece of parchment paper to fit along the bottom and up two sides of a 9- × 9-inch (2.5 L) baking pan. (The parchment extending up the sides will be used to lift the square out of the pan once baked.) Place the crust ingredients in a medium bowl and thoroughly mix until well combined. Spread into the baking pan and pack it down firmly and evenly.

Place an oven rack in the middle position. Preheat the oven to 375°F (190°C). To make the filling, place the eggs in a mixing bowl and beat well. Mix in the brown sugar, granulated sugar, vanilla, cinnamon, nutmeg and cloves. Add the pecans, coconut and currants, blending well. Spread the mixture evenly over the crust. Bake for 25 minutes, or until the filling is set and is a rich brown color on top. Cool on a baking rack to room temperature.

Cut around the outer edges of the square to loosen it from the pan. Use the parchment paper to lift the square out of the pan. Wrap well and refrigerate. To serve, cut with a sharp, serrated knife into 1½-inch (4 cm) squares.

SHORTBREAD COOKIES TWO WAYS

preparation time ·	60 minutes	
cooking time ·	20 minutes per sheet of cookies	
makes ·	48 cookies	

Divide this basic shortbread dough in two and flavor each half in a separate, decadent way!

ERIC'S OPTIONS

Make some plain shortbread using the basic dough. Roll into balls as described in the recipes or shape into crescents. Bake as described in the recipes, ensuring you chill the rolled cookies first. Roll the cookies in icing sugar just before serving, if desired.

BASIC DOUGH

1½ cups	butter, softened	375 mL
¾ cup	icing sugar	175 mL
1 tsp	pure vanilla extract	5 mL
2¼ cups	all-purpose flour	560 mL
⅓ cup	cornstarch	75 mL
2 tsp	finely grated orange zest	10 mL

RUM AND CURRANT

⅓ cup	currants	75 mL
¼ cup	rum	60 mL
for rolling	icing sugar (optional)	for rolling

PISTACHIO AND CRANBERRY

¼ cup	unsalted, shelled pistachios (see Note)	60 mL
¼–⅓ cup	cranberry sauce	60–75 mL

Bake for larger Good Supper Group 18/1/14

Place the butter, icing sugar and vanilla in the bowl of a stand mixer fitted with the paddle attachment. Beat until well combined and very light. Beat in the flour, cornstarch and orange zest. Flour your hands and gather the dough into a large ball. Set on a lightly floured surface and cut the dough in half. Wrap each half in plastic wrap and set aside until needed.

Place the currants and rum in a small bowl and steep for 2 hours. Drain the currants well (save the leftover rum for another use, such as rum balls). Line a baking sheet with parchment paper.

Place one of the balls of shortbread dough in a mixing bowl. Add the currants and orange zest and mix well. Roll into 1-inch (2.5 cm) balls and place on the baking sheet, spacing each cookie about 2 inches (5 cm) apart. Refrigerate the cookies for at least 20 minutes.

Preheat the oven to 300°F (150°C). Bake the cookies for 20 minutes, or until very pale golden around the edges. If desired, roll the cookies in icing sugar just before serving.

Line a baking sheet with parchment paper. Place the pistachios on a cutting board and finely chop them (there should be very small pieces of pistachio still visible). Place the second half of the shortbread dough in a mixing bowl. Add the chopped pistachios, mixing them in well. Roll into 1-inch (2.5 cm) balls and place on the baking sheet, spacing them about 2 inches (5 cm) apart. Use a floured finger to make a deep dimple in the center of each ball. Fill the dimple with a small spoonful, about ¼ tsp (1 mL), of the cranberry sauce. Refrigerate the cookies for at least 20 minutes.

Preheat the oven to 300°F (150°C). Bake the cookies for 20 minutes, or until very pale golden around the edges.

Once baked, store the cookies in a tightly sealed container for up to 2 weeks, or freeze them for up to a month. Cool the baked cookies on a rack to room temperature before storing.

NOTE
Shelled unsalted pistachios are sold at bulk food stores or in the bulk food section of most supermarkets. Also, remember to steep the currants ahead of time so they'll be ready to use when you are making the dough.

WHITE CHOCOLATE, CRANBERRY and PECAN CLUSTERS

preparation time	·	20 minutes
cooking time	·	3–4 minutes
makes	·	20 clusters

Sweet, festive treats for your family or to package up and give as a gift.

ERIC'S OPTIONS
Instead of white chocolate, use dark or milk chocolate. Replace the pecans with roasted unsalted cashews.

⅔ lb	white chocolate, coarsely chopped	350 g
1 cup	dried cranberries	250 mL
¾ cup	pecan halves	175 mL

Line a baking sheet with parchment paper and set aside. Melt the chocolate in a heatproof bowl over simmering water. Remove from the heat. Mix in the cranberries and pecans. Drop heaping tablespoonfuls (15+ mL) of the mixture onto the prepared baking sheet. Refrigerate until the clusters are set. Store in a tightly sealed container at cool room temperature. If stacking the clusters, be sure to place a sheet of parchment paper between each layer.

CREAMY CHEESECAKE with EGGNOG and SPICE

preparation time	·	25 minutes
cooking time	·	80 minutes
makes	·	12 servings

Flavored with a classic seasonal drink and an aromatic mix of spices, this creamy cake is perfect for holiday entertaining—particularly since it can be made up to two days ahead.

ERIC'S OPTIONS

Chocolate lovers may want to substitute chocolate cookie crumbs for the graham cracker crumbs in the crust.

CRUST

1¼ cups	graham cracker crumbs	310 mL
⅓ cup	granulated sugar	75 mL
¼ cup	butter, melted	60 mL

BATTER

3	8 oz (250 g) bricks cream cheese, softened	3
1 cup	granulated sugar	250 mL
1 cup	eggnog	250 mL
1 Tbsp	all-purpose flour	15 mL
3	large eggs	3
1 tsp	rum extract	5 mL
½ tsp	ground cinnamon, plus some for sprinkling	2 mL
½ tsp	ground nutmeg, plus some for sprinkling	2 mL
pinch	ground cloves	pinch
1 cup	whipping cream, whipped	250 mL

Cut a circle of parchment paper to fit the bottom of a 10-inch (3 L) springform cake pan. For the crust, combine the graham cracker crumbs, sugar and butter in a bowl. Pack the crust mixture evenly into the bottom of the pan and partially up the sides.

Preheat the oven to 325°F (160°C) and place 1 rack in the lower position and another in the middle position. To make the batter, place the cream cheese and sugar in a bowl and beat with an electric mixer until lightened. Beat in the eggnog and flour until smooth. Beat in the eggs, one at a time. Stir in the rum extract, cinnamon, nutmeg and cloves. Pour the batter into the prepared cake pan. Place a shallow pan of water on the bottom rack of the oven; the steam rising from it will help prevent the cheesecake from cracking as it bakes. Set the cake on the rack above the water and bake 80 minutes, or until the cake jiggles slightly only in the very center. Cool the cake on a baking rack for 15 minutes, and then run a sharp, thin and wet paring knife around the edges of the cake to a depth of 1 inch (2.5 cm). This will also prevent the cake from cracking as it cools and contracts. Cool the cake to room temperature. Cover and refrigerate in the pan for at least 3 hours.

When you're ready to serve the cake, run a wet paring knife completely around the outer edges of the pan to loosen the cake from the sides. Remove the cake pan's outer ring.

Cut the cake into wedges and set on plates. Top each wedge with a dollop or piped spiral of the whipped cream. Sprinkle the whipped cream lightly with cinnamon and nutmeg and serve.

DARK BELGIAN HOT CHOCOLATE
with CANDY CANES

preparation time	·	10 minutes
cooking time	·	about 5 minutes
makes	·	4–6 servings

This intensely chocolate drink, adorned with a candy cane stir stick, is fun to present and makes a fine way to cap off a snowy Christmas Eve.

ERIC'S OPTIONS
To make this less rich, replace the cream with milk. For a sweeter taste, use milk chocolate instead of dark chocolate.

3 cups	milk	750 mL
1 cup	light (10%) cream	250 mL
5 oz	dark Belgian chocolate, coarsely chopped	150 g
¼ cup	granulated sugar, or to taste	60 mL
½ tsp	pure vanilla extract	2 mL
½ tsp	ground cinnamon	2 mL
¼ cup	finely chopped white chocolate (about 1 oz/25 g)	60 mL
4–6	candy canes	4–6

Place the milk and cream in a pot over medium heat; bring it to just below a boil. Add the dark chocolate, sugar, vanilla and cinnamon, stirring continually until the chocolate is melted and well incorporated into the milk and cream. Whisk for 1 to 2 minutes more, until it's foamy on the surface. Pour into mugs, sprinkle with white chocolate and place a candy cane in each drink.

MENUS

HOLIDAY SEASON DINNER BUFFET

There are two strategies you can employ with this splendid menu. You could serve it as is and invite 8 guests, storing any leftover cookies away for another holiday meal. Or you could host a potluck dinner buffet for a larger group and ask guests to bring an appetizer, main course, side dish or dessert to supplement this menu. If you have a very large crowd over, expand the recipes in the menu as needed. Serve the chicken alongside some steamed rice.

- Herbed Goat Cheese Logs (page 190)
- Cranberry Maple Chicken (page 196)
- Broccoli Florets with Roasted Peppers (page 206)
- Shortbread Cookies Two Ways (page 210)

CHRISTMAS EVE DINNER

My French Canadian mother instilled in me the tradition of serving tourtière on Christmas Eve, something I carried on when I got married and became a father. This meat pie is usually made with pork, but over the years I've played around with its filling ingredients. In my first book, *Everyone Can Cook*, I published a recipe for the one I most often serve, made with beef, veal and pork. There is also a vegetarian version of tourtière in that book. In my third book, *Everyone Can Cook Appetizers*, I included a recipe for tourtière phyllo bundles, a bite-sized version of the dish.

Last year I decided to see what tourtière would taste like when made with ground turkey, and I added yams and cranberries for seasonal flair. The results were delicious and the recipe makes a nice main course, served with a simple green salad, for this festive menu for 6.

- Shrimp Bisque with Curry (page 186)
- Turkey Tourtière with Yams and Cranberries (page 200)
- Dark Belgian Hot Chocolate with Candy Canes (page 216)

Continued on the next page . . .

CHRISTMAS DINNER

Cornish hens are juicy, tasty and a fine alternative to turkey for Christmas dinner. They roast fairly quickly and the only carving required, besides cutting them in half and putting them in the roasting pan, is on the dinner plate. In this menu that serves 8, the hens are accompanied with a pair of vegetable side dishes and a fruit- and nut-filled salad, followed by a cheesecake. All can be readied partially or entirely in advance. If you're serving only 4, the recipes are easily halved, except for the cheesecake—but you certainly won't mind having any leftovers to enjoy the next day.

- Roast Cornish Hens Glazed with Maple and Dijon (page 202)
- Sautéed Brussels Sprouts with Ginger, Red Pepper and Orange (page 204)
- Spiced Yam Rounds (page 207)
- Wild Rice Salad with Mixed Fruit and Nuts (page 194)
- Creamy Cheesecake with Eggnog and Spice (page 214)

HOLIDAY LUNCH

For many, the period between Christmas Day and New Year's Eve is a time for relaxing and socializing with family and friends. People often have a few days off work, the pressure associated with the buildup to Christmas is gone, and homes are still festively decorated and welcoming—a great time for visiting if there ever was one. This lunch menu, which serves 6, is designed to use up any tasty bites left over from holiday feasting. The squares in this menu can be baked earlier in the month, frozen and enjoyed throughout the season.

- Mixed Salad Greens with Pear and Pomegranate (page 192)
- Turkey, Vegetable and Bow-Tie Pasta Soup (page 188)
- Pecan, Coconut and Currant Squares (page 208)

RINGING IN THE NEW YEAR

CHAPTER EIGHT

SPARKLING LEMON
POMEGRANATE SPRITZERS

preparation time · 10 minutes
cooking time · a few minutes
makes · 6 servings

Here's a fizzy drink that's fun to serve and good for you, as it's rich in antioxidants and vitamin C from the pomegranate juice and lemon.

ERIC'S OPTIONS
For added pizzazz, freeze 2 to 3 blueberries in each slot of your ice cube trays when you're making ice cubes and use these in the drinks.

2 cups	cold water	500 mL
½ cup	granulated sugar	125 mL
1 cup	fresh lemon juice	250 mL
½ cup	pomegranate juice	125 mL
2 cups	sparkling wine or soda water	500 mL
3	lemon slices, halved	3
6	fresh mint sprigs	6

Place ½ cup (125 mL) of the water and the sugar in a small pot over medium-high heat and bring to a boil. Cook, stirring, until the sugar has completely dissolved and the liquid is clear, about 1 to 2 minutes. Pour into a 4-cup (1 L) container. Mix in the remaining 1½ cups (375 mL) of cold water, lemon juice and pomegranate juice. Cover and refrigerate until needed. (Can be prepared a day or two in advance.)

To serve, assemble 6 tall 8 oz (250 mL) glasses and put 4 to 5 ice cubes in each. Divide the lemon/pomegranate mixture among them and top up each glass with the sparkling wine or soda water. Garnish each drink with a half lemon slice and a mint sprig.

NEW YEAR'S DAY PUNCH

preparation time	·	5 minutes
cooking time	·	none
makes	·	about 14 cups (3.5 L), about 16 servings

Six kinds of fruit—cranberry, pear, apple, blueberry, orange and lemon—combine in a pleasing punch to serve a New Year's Day crowd. The molded ice ring looks beautiful and keeps the punch cold.

ERIC'S OPTIONS

For an alcoholic punch, use sparkling wine instead of soda water. For a sweeter punch, replace 3 cups (750 mL) of the soda water with 3 cups (750 mL) of ginger ale.

1 cup	frozen blueberries	250 mL
6	thin orange slices, each cut in half	6
6	thin lemon slices, each cut in half	6
12	fresh mint sprigs	12
4 cups	chilled cranberry juice	1 L
2 cups	chilled apple cider or juice	500 mL
2 cups	chilled pear juice	500 mL
6 cups	cold soda water	1.5 L

Place the blueberries, orange and lemon slices and mint in a 9-inch (3 L) tube (ringed) pan. Fill the pan half full with cold water; freeze until solid. Combine the cranberry juice, apple cider and pear juice in a punch bowl. Unmold the ring of frozen fruit and mint and place it in the punch bowl, where it will keep your punch nice and cold. Pour in the soda water and serve.

MIXED FRUIT COCKTAIL in GINGER SYRUP

preparation time	·	15 minutes
cooking time	·	3–4 minutes
makes	·	8 servings

The fresh ginger gives this cocktail an added depth of flavor.

ERIC'S OPTIONS
You can prepare the fruit cocktail and syrup the night before. Keep the fruit cocktail in the refrigerator; the syrup can be left out at room temperature. Combine them an hour before serving. Substitute other sliced or whole fresh fruit for those called for, such as papaya for the mango, or blueberries for the grapes; use fruit of mixed colors to keep the fruit cocktail visually interesting.

½ cup	granulated sugar	125 mL
½ cup	water	125 mL
1 Tbsp	finely grated fresh ginger	15 mL
1	medium ripe mango, peeled and cubed	1
2–3	medium kiwi, peeled, halved and sliced	2–3
16–20	fresh strawberries, hulled and sliced	16–20
2–3	mandarin oranges, peeled and separated into segments	2–3
1 cup	purple or red seedless grapes	250 mL
1 Tbsp	chopped fresh mint	15 mL

Place the sugar, water and ginger in a small pot and bring to a boil. Stir until the sugar dissolves; remove from the heat and cool to room temperature. Place the mango, kiwi, strawberries, oranges and grapes in a bowl. Toss in the mint. Pour in the ginger syrup. Refrigerate to let the fruit steep in the syrup for 1 hour before serving. Set the fruit on the table with small bowls alongside and allow diners to help themselves.

CURING A NEW YEAR'S EVE HANGOVER

There is a surefire way to cure a hangover: don't drink the night before, or be very modest in the amount you consume. If it's too late for that advice, here are some things that might minimize its effects.

Have plenty to eat before you drink and during the evening

If you start drinking on an empty stomach you can quickly get past the tipping point of no return. Feasting before and during your New Year's Eve night of partying should help reduce your alcoholic intake and slow down the rate of absorption.

Keep hydrated

Drinking water abundantly during the evening can help to limit the dehydrating effects of alcohol. After you grab that cab and are safely home, drink another bucket of water before you go to bed and another bucketful when you wake up.

Don't pop painkillers

This may sound surprising, but some health authorities advise that taking a lot of over-the-counter painkillers can irritate an already sensitive stomach and make you feel worse.

Have a hearty breakfast, a brisk walk and a nap

A good breakfast after a long night of revelry will provide a much-needed energy boost and get you on the road to recovery. Drink fruit juices with the meal to get rehydrated and replace lost vitamins. Coffee may wake you up, but it has similar dehydrating effects as alcohol and should not be overconsumed. After breakfast, go for a long walk to clear your head, follow that with a nap, and by dinnertime you should be in fairly good shape to enjoy New Year's Day dinner.

MORNING GLORY PANCAKES

preparation time · 10 minutes
cooking time · 4–5 minutes per batch
makes · about 18 pancakes

Get a tasty start to the New Year with these pancakes flavored with orange and coconut. The generous amount of baking powder used in the batter ensures they are light and fluffy. Serve them with softened butter and a jug of maple syrup.

ERIC'S OPTIONS
For an extra special touch, serve the pancakes with maple cranberry sauce. Place 1½ cups (375 mL) fresh or frozen cranberries in a pot with 1 cup (250 mL) maple syrup, ¼ cup (60 mL) orange juice, and pinches of ground cinnamon, clove and nutmeg. Gently simmer 20 to 25 minutes, or until the cranberries are tender. Serve warm or at room temperature.

3	large eggs	3
¾ cup	2% milk	175 mL
¾ cup	orange juice	175 mL
2 tsp	finely grated orange zest	10 mL
1¾ cups	all-purpose flour	425 mL
⅓ cup	granulated sugar	75 mL
2 Tbsp	baking powder	30 mL
½ cup	medium, unsweetened coconut flakes	125 mL
¼ tsp	salt	1 mL

Whisk together the eggs, milk, orange juice and orange zest in a bowl. Combine the flour, sugar, baking powder, coconut and salt in a second bowl. Add the dry ingredients to the wet and stir until just combined. Let rest 5 minutes (it will become bubbly), and give it a few stirs before cooking. Preheat the oven to 200°F (95°C).

Preheat a nonstick griddle to medium or medium-high heat. Lightly coat with oil or cooking spray. With a small ladle, pour 4-inch (10 cm) rounds of batter on the griddle, leaving a 2-inch (5 cm) space between each pancake. Flip the pancakes when the top becomes speckled with bubbles. Continue cooking until the underside is browned and the center of the pancake springs back when touched. Keep warm in the oven until all are done.

PORK and OAT SAUSAGE PATTIES

preparation time · 15 minutes
cooking time · 6–8 minutes per batch
makes · 12 patties

Savory, hand-formed sausage patties are a great side dish with eggs or pancakes.

ERIC'S OPTIONS
The patties can be mixed and shaped the day before, refrigerated and cooked when needed.

1¼ lb	ground pork	625 g
1	large egg, beaten	1
½ cup	quick cooking oats	125 mL
½ tsp	crumbled dried sage	2 mL
¼ tsp	paprika	1 mL
¾ tsp	salt	4 mL
½ tsp	freshly ground black pepper	2 mL
2 Tbsp	vegetable oil	30 mL

Preheat the oven to 200°F (95°C). Place the pork, egg, oats, sage, paprika, salt and pepper in a bowl and mix until just combined. Moisten your hands with cold water. Divide the pork mixture into 12 equal balls and shape each ball into a ¾-inch-thick (2 cm) patty. Heat the oil in a large skillet over medium or medium-high heat. Cook the patties in batches for 3 to 4 minutes per side, or until entirely cooked through and the juices run clear with no hint of pink. Reserve the cooked patties in the oven while frying up the rest.

PARSNIP and PEAR SOUP with BALSAMIC-MAPLE DRIZZLE

preparation time · 15 minutes
cooking time · about 20 minutes
makes · 6 servings

The humble parsnip offers a surprising array of flavors—nutty, sweet, earthy and almost peppery. In this recipe they are whirled into a silky soup flavored with pear. The sweet-sour balsamic vinegar and maple syrup drizzle is the finishing touch.

ERIC'S OPTIONS

The soup can be made a day or two in advance, cooled to room temperature and refrigerated. Reheat and drizzle when needed. For an added touch of richness, after drizzling with maple/balsamic mixture, top each bowl of soup with 1 Tbsp (15 mL) or so of crumbled blue cheese.

3 Tbsp	butter	45 mL
1½ lb	parsnips, peeled, halved lengthwise and sliced	750 g
½	medium onion, chopped	½
2 Tbsp	all-purpose flour	30 mL
4 cups	chicken or vegetable stock	1 L
1	ripe medium pear, peeled, cored and cubed	1
2 tsp	chopped fresh rosemary	10 mL
to taste	salt and white pepper	to taste
2 tsp	maple syrup	10 mL
2 tsp	balsamic vinegar	10 mL

Melt the butter in a large pot over medium heat. Add the parsnips and onion and cook until softened, about 4 to 5 minutes. Mix in the flour and cook 1 to 2 minutes more. While stirring, very slowly pour in the stock. Mix in the pear and rosemary. Bring to a gentle simmer and cook the soup until the parsnips are very tender, about 15 minutes. Purée the soup in a food processor or blender, or in the pot with an immersion blender. Thin with a little more stock if too thick. Return the soup to a simmer; season with salt and pepper.

Combine the maple syrup and balsamic vinegar in a small bowl. Ladle the soup into heated bowls. Use a small spoon to drizzle the top of each serving with a little of the maple/balsamic mixture, using a swirling motion. Serve immediately.

ONION SOUP with CRUMBLED STILTON

preparation time	·	20 minutes
cooking time	·	30 minutes
makes	·	6 servings

The sherry raises this delicious onion soup up a notch, and the blue cheese topping finishes the job!

ERIC'S OPTIONS
The soup can be made a day or two in advance, cooled to room temperature, covered and refrigerated until needed. Top with the cheese and green onion after reheating. Instead of Stilton, top the soup with another, good-quality type of blue cheese, such as roquefort.

3 Tbsp	butter	45 mL
4	medium onions, cut in half and thinly sliced	4
2	garlic cloves, finely chopped	2
2 Tbsp	tomato paste	30 mL
6 cups	beef stock	1.5 L
1 tsp	dried tarragon	5 mL
1	bay leaf	1
⅓ cup	dry sherry	75 mL
to taste	salt and freshly ground black pepper	to taste
¼ lb	Stilton cheese, crumbled	125 g
2	green onions, thinly sliced	2

Melt the butter in a pot over medium heat. Add the onions and cook, stirring occasionally, for 10 minutes, or until they are caramelized and sticky. Add the garlic and tomato paste and cook 1 minute more. Add the stock, tarragon and bay leaf and simmer the soup for 20 minutes. Stir in the sherry, salt and pepper. To serve, ladle the soup into warmed bowls and top each serving with the crumbled Stilton and green onions.

EMERALD and WHITE JADE SOUP

preparation time · 10 minutes
cooking time · about 5 minutes
makes · 8 servings

Begin a Chinese New Year celebration with this simple but flavorful soup. In China, emeralds and white jade are prized gemstones and they are represented in this soup by the tofu and spinach.

ERIC'S OPTIONS
If you like things spicy, omit the black pepper and add 1 to 2 tsp (5 to 10 mL) hot, Asian-style chili sauce to the soup when bringing it to a simmer.

7 cups	chicken stock	1.75 L
2 Tbsp	chopped fresh ginger	30 mL
3	garlic cloves, crushed	3
2 Tbsp	light soy sauce	30 mL
to taste	freshly ground black pepper	to taste
2	10 oz (300 g) pkgs soft tofu, cut into ½-inch (1 cm) cubes	2
4 cups	baby spinach, stems removed, leaves thickly sliced	1 L

Place the stock, ginger, garlic, soy sauce and pepper in a pot and bring to a simmer. Cook for 2 to 3 minutes. Divide the tofu among 8 heated shallow soup bowls. Swirl the spinach into the simmering stock and cook for 1 minute, until just wilted but still vibrant green. Ladle the soup into the bowls; serve immediately.

SHRIMP COCKTAIL CANAPÉS

preparation time	·	20 minutes
cooking time	·	none
makes	·	24 canapés

These delicious little canapés featuring the elements found in a shrimp cocktail are handily served on small rounds of rye bread—great for a stand-up party.

ERIC'S OPTIONS
Use store-bought cocktail sauce or make your own by combining ½ cup (125 mL) ketchup, 1 Tbsp (15 mL) prepared horseradish, ½ tsp (2 mL) hot pepper sauce, 1 tsp (5 mL) Worcestershire sauce and 1 Tbsp (15 mL) fresh lemon juice in a small bowl. Stir in salt and freshly ground black pepper to taste. Chill well before using.

24	cocktail rye bread rounds (see Note)	24
½ cup	spreadable cream cheese	125 mL
1½ cups	mixed baby salad greens	375 mL
½ lb	small cooked, fresh or frozen (thawed) salad shrimp, patted dry	250 g
⅓ cup	cocktail sauce	75 mL
24	small parsley sprigs	24
for garnish	twirls of lemon zest (see Note)	for garnish

Spread a thin layer of cream cheese on each piece of rye bread. Top with a few leaves of the salad greens. Place 2 to 3 shrimp on each canapé. (Can be made to this point several hours in advance. Cover and refrigerate until needed.) Top the shrimp with a small spoonful of the cocktail sauce. Garnish each canapé with a parsley sprig and a few twirls of lemon zest and serve.

NOTE
Ready-to-use rye bread rounds are sold in plastic tubs at most supermarket delicatessens. If unavailable, use a round cookie cutter to cut thin slices of rye bread into 1½-inch (4 cm) rounds, or use a small, sturdy round cracker as the base for these canapés. I used a lemon zester to make the thin twirls of lemon zest garnishing the canapés.

OYSTERS on the HALF SHELL with DILL RED PEPPER VINAIGRETTE

preparation time	·	30 minutes
cooking time	·	none
makes	·	6–8 servings

A tangy, green- and red-flecked vinaigrette tops these small, slurping-size raw oysters. Buy oysters with tightly closed shells that feel heavy for their size, an indication they still contain their precious juice.

ERIC'S OPTIONS

You can make and refrigerate the vinaigrette several hours in advance of serving. Although oysters always taste best when shucked and served immediately, you can shuck them 1 to 2 hours before serving, place on a baking sheet, cover and refrigerate until you're ready to place them on the serving tray and top with the vinaigrette. You may wish to do this if your shucking skills aren't great and you want to get the kitchen and yourself cleaned up before guests arrive for the party.

2 Tbsp	white wine vinegar	30 mL
1 tsp	Dijon mustard	5 mL
⅓ cup	olive oil	75 mL
2 Tbsp	finely chopped red bell pepper	30 mL
1 tsp	chopped fresh dill	5 mL
½ tsp	hot pepper sauce	2 mL
pinch	granulated sugar	pinch
to taste	salt and freshly ground black pepper	to taste
24	small, fresh oysters, scrubbed well	24

Place the vinegar and mustard in a medium bowl and whisk to combine. Slowly whisk in the oil. Mix in the red pepper, dill, hot sauce, sugar, salt and pepper. Refrigerate until needed.

Place an oyster on a slightly damp kitchen towel, cupped side down with the hinged end facing you. Hold it in place with another kitchen towel. Insert the point of your oyster knife into the hinge of the shells. Work the knife in ¼ inch (6 mm), and then twist it to pry the shell open. Slide the knife across the top shell and remove the shell. Slide the knife under the oyster to detach it from the bottom shell. Remove any shell fragments. Place the oyster on a serving tray filled with crushed ice. Repeat with the remaining oysters. Spoon some vinaigrette on each oyster and serve.

ROASTED LOBSTER TAILS

preparation time · 20 minutes
cooking time · 8–10 minutes
makes · 6 servings

This is a restaurant-style way of preparing and cooking lobster tails, where the meat is pulled out of the shell when raw, artfully set on top of the shell, basted with flavored butter, and roasted. Create a "surf and turf" New Year's Eve dinner by serving each lobster tail with a small, grilled or pan-seared beef tenderloin steak.

ERIC'S OPTIONS

The lobster tails can be made oven-ready several hours in advance; cover and refrigerate until you're ready to roast them. Add 1 minute to the cooking time as the lobster will be quite cold. For added richness, serve each lobster tail with a small dish of melted butter for dipping.

6	5–6 oz (150–175 g) frozen lobster tails, thawed and patted dry	6
3 Tbsp	melted butter	45 mL
1 Tbsp	fresh lemon juice	15 mL
2 tsp	chopped fresh parsley	10 mL
1	garlic clove, crushed	1
pinch	paprika and cayenne pepper	pinch

Preheat the oven to 425°F (220°C). Line a baking sheet with parchment paper. Place 1 of the lobster tails on a work surface. With a sharp knife, make a lengthwise cut down the middle of the top shell, cutting three-quarters of the way into the flesh, but not through the bottom part of the shell. Spread the cut side of the shell open. Carefully pull out the tail meat. Close the shell and set on the baking sheet. Fan the meat, cut side up, on top of the shell. Repeat with the remaining lobster tails. Whisk the remaining ingredients in a small bowl. Brush the mixture on the lobster meat. Roast the lobster tails 8 to 10 minutes, or until just cooked through.

SHRIMP and MIXED VEGETABLE CHOW MEIN

preparation time · 25 minutes
cooking time · 5–6 minutes
makes · 6–8 servings

Long noodles, such as the ones featured in this colorful dish, are always part of a Chinese New Year meal. They symbolize long life—a benefit thought to be achieved by consuming them. That's certainly not a hardship when the noodles are surrounded with tasty shrimp and fresh and flavorful vegetables.

ERIC'S OPTIONS
If you like things spicy, add 1 to 2 tsp (5 to 10 mL) hot Asian-style chili sauce to the wok or skillet when you're adding the soy sauce, stock and shrimp.

1	10 oz (300 g) package fresh Chinese-style egg noodles	1
1 Tbsp	sesame oil	15 mL
2 Tbsp	vegetable oil	30 mL
2	garlic cloves, finely chopped	2
1 Tbsp	chopped fresh ginger	15 mL
1	medium green bell pepper, cubed	1
3	baby bok choy, trimmed and chopped	3
1	14 oz (398 mL) can young (baby) corn, drained well	1
1	8 oz (250 mL) can sliced water chestnuts, drained well	1
¼ cup	light soy sauce	60 mL
¼ cup	chicken or vegetable stock	60 mL
24–30	medium cooked, peeled shrimp (see Note)	24–30
2 cups	bean sprouts	500 mL
3	green onions, cut into 1-inch (2.5 cm) pieces	3

Continued on the next page . . .

Cook the noodles for 45 seconds in boiling water, or until just tender. Drain well, cool in ice-cold water, and drain well again. Place the noodles in a bowl and toss with the sesame oil.

Heat the vegetable oil in a wok or large skillet over medium-high heat. Add the garlic, ginger, and green pepper and stir-fry 1 minute. Add the bok choy, baby corn and water chestnuts and stir-fry 1 more minute. Add the soy sauce, stock and shrimp and bring the liquid to a simmer. Mix in the noodles, bean sprouts and green onions; gently toss and heat the noodles through 2 to 3 minutes. Transfer to a large platter and serve.

NOTE
Fresh Chinese-style egg noodles can be found at Asian markets and most super-markets. Cooked, peeled shrimp are available in the seafood department of most supermarkets.

CHINESE-STYLE BARBECUE CHICKEN

preparation time · 20 minutes plus marinating time
cooking time · 90 minutes
makes · 6–8 buffet-sized servings

An aromatic, richly flavored and beautifully glazed chicken that's cooked in the oven.

ERIC'S OPTIONS
Instead of a whole chicken, use 4 chicken legs, or 4 bone-in breasts. Reduce the cooking time to 45 to 50 minutes, as the pieces will cook more quickly than a whole chicken.

3 lb	whole chicken	1.5 kg
¼ cup	soy sauce	60 mL
¼ cup	ketchup	60 mL
¼ cup	dry sherry or Chinese cooking wine	60 mL
2 tsp	grated fresh ginger	10 mL
2	garlic cloves, minced	2
2 Tbsp	honey	30 mL
½ tsp	five spice powder	2 mL
½ tsp	freshly ground black pepper	2 mL
for garnish	halved orange slices and sliced green onion	for garnish

Wash the chicken and pat dry with paper towels. Whisk together the remaining ingredients, except oranges and green onions, in a medium bowl. Add the chicken and turn to coat. Cover, refrigerate and marinate the chicken for 4 hours or overnight, turning and brushing with the marinade occasionally.

Preheat the oven to 350°F (180°C). Place chicken breast side up in a shallow-sided roasting pan lined with parchment. Tuck the wings under the body; tie the legs together. Brush the chicken with the marinade. Roast, basting it every 20 minutes, for 90 minutes, or until the temperature in the center of the thigh, not touching the bone, registers 170°F (77°C) on an instant-read meat thermometer. Set the chicken on a plate, tent with foil and let it rest for 10 minutes. After resting time, with a sharp carving knife, remove the leg and wing on 1 side of the bird. Cut the leg into drumstick and thigh pieces, and then thinly slice the meat from the bone. To carve the breast, make very thin, slightly angled, vertical slices that run parallel to the breastbone. Repeat on the other side of the bird. Arrange the meat on a platter, garnish with orange slices and green onion and serve.

BEEF TENDERLOIN STEAKS with CRAB-STUFFED MUSHROOMS

preparation time	·	20 minutes
cooking time	·	about 20 minutes
makes	·	6 servings

Here's a tasty version of "surf and turf"—an ultratender steak paired with crab-stuffed mushroom caps. Add a baked potato and some buttery green beans or zucchini to each plate, and dinner is ready. For tips on cooking the meat, see Grilling the Perfect Steak on page 101.

ERIC'S OPTIONS
Instead of tenderloin, use any tender steak, such as rib-eye or top sirloin medallions. Instead of crab in the mushroom stuffing, use an equal amount of finely chopped cooked salad shrimp.

¾ cup	canned or fresh crabmeat	175 mL
⅓ cup	spreadable cream cheese	75 mL
1	garlic clove, crushed	1
1	green onion, thinly sliced	1
½ tsp	hot pepper sauce	2 mL
to taste	salt, freshly ground black pepper and lemon juice	to taste
18	medium white or brown mushrooms, stems removed	18
¼ cup	freshly grated Parmesan cheese	60 mL
6	5 oz (150 g) beef tenderloin steaks	6

Line a 9- × 13-inch (3.5 L) baking dish with parchment paper. Place the crabmeat, cream cheese, garlic, green onion, hot pepper sauce, salt, pepper and lemon juice in a bowl and mix well to combine. Stuff the crab mixture inside the mushroom caps. (The mushrooms can be stuffed in the morning, covered and refrigerated. Add a few minutes cooking time if you cook the mushrooms from a chilled state.) Set the mushroom caps in the baking dish; sprinkle with the Parmesan cheese.

Preheat the oven to 350°F (180°C). Preheat your grill to medium-high. Bake the mushrooms 15 to 20 minutes, or until tender and the stuffing is golden brown.

While the mushrooms bake, season the steaks with salt and pepper. Lightly oil the bars of the grill. Grill the steaks, 2 to 3 minutes per side for rare, and 3 to 4 minutes for medium rare to medium. Serve the steaks and mushrooms together.

ROAST STRIP LOIN with DIJON and HERBES de PROVENCE

preparation time · 10 minutes
cooking time · depends on desired doneness
makes · 6 servings

Strip loin roasts can vary in thickness depending on what end of the loin they were cut from and that can affect cooking time. I've given approximate cooking times below, but it's best to use an instant-read meat thermometer, inserted into the center of the thickest part of the roast, to gauge doneness. Cook the meat to 125°F (50°C) for rare, 130°F to 135°F (55°C to 57°C) for medium rare, 140°F (60°C) for medium. Remember that the meat will continue to cook when you let it rest before slicing.

ERIC'S OPTIONS
If you prefer its coarser texture, use whole-grain Dijon mustard instead of the smooth type of Dijon. If you don't use alcohol, use another ½ cup (125 mL) of beef stock to make the jus.

3 lb	strip loin roast	1.5 kg
2 Tbsp	Dijon mustard	30 mL
1 Tbsp	herbes de Provence	15 mL
to taste	coarse sea salt and coarsely ground black pepper	to taste
½ cup	red wine	125 mL
2½ cups	beef stock	625 mL

Preheat the oven to 450°F (230°C). Place the beef, fat side up, in a medium-sized roasting pan. Combine the mustard and herbes de Provence in a small bowl. Brush the beef with the mustard mixture; season with salt and pepper. Roast the beef for 20 minutes. Lower the oven temperature to 325°F (160°C) and cook the roast to the desired doneness, approximately 30 to 40 minutes for rare and 40 to 50 minutes for medium rare to medium.

Set the roast on a plate, cover with foil and let it rest for 10 minutes before carving it into thin slices.

To make jus, set the roasting pan on the stovetop over medium-high heat. Add the wine and bring to a simmer, scraping the bottom of the pan to lift off the tasty brown bits. Add the stock and simmer a few minutes more. Pour the jus into a sauceboat and serve alongside the beef.

NO-FUSS YORKSHIRE PUDDINGS

preparation time · 10 minutes
cooking time · 45–50 minutes
makes · 12 puddings

This easy technique for making Yorkshire pudding was shared with me by a colleague years ago and I've used it ever since. Some Yorkshire pudding recipes require you to heat the oiled pan until smoking hot before pouring in the batter; in this method you simply pour the batter into a well-greased muffin tin, no preheating required. The puddings puff beautifully. Make sure you use a good-quality, nonstick muffin tin. If you use an old, well-worn pan, the puddings may stick.

ERIC'S OPTIONS
The Yorkshire puddings can be made the morning of the day you intend to serve them. After removing them from the pan, place on a baking sheet and cool to room temperature. Cover and keep at room temperature until needed. To reheat, place in a 325°F (160°C) oven for 5 to 10 minutes.

6	large eggs	6
¾ cup	milk	175 mL
¾ cup	water	175 mL
to taste	salt and white pepper	to taste
pinch	nutmeg	pinch
1½ cups	all-purpose flour	375 mL
for greasing	vegetable oil spray	for greasing

Preheat the oven to 450°F (230°C). Beat the eggs in a bowl until the yolks and whites are well blended. Whisk in the milk, water, salt, pepper and nutmeg. Whisk in the flour until just combined (it's okay if there are a few lumps). Thoroughly grease a nonstick 12-cup muffin tin with vegetable oil spray. Pour in the batter, filling each cup almost to the top. Bake for 10 minutes. Reduce the heat to 325°F (160°C) and bake 35 to 40 minutes more, or until the Yorkshire puddings are puffed and golden and almost dry in the center. Set on a baking rack to cool for a few minutes before removing them from the pan.

THE EMPEROR'S FRIED RICE

preparation time ·	25 minutes	
cooking time ·	about 10 minutes	
makes ·	6–8 servings	

Tender pork, succulent shrimp, crisp snow peas and crunchy, rich cashews make this version of fried rice a regal one.

ERIC'S OPTIONS
If you prefer the taste of chicken, replace the pork tenderloin with ¾ lb (375 g) boneless, skinless chicken breast. Slice and stir-fry it as described for the pork.

3 Tbsp	vegetable oil	45 mL
¾ lb	pork tenderloin, halved lengthwise and thinly sliced	375 g
½	medium onion, finely chopped	½
½	medium green bell pepper, finely chopped	½
16	snow peas, thickly sliced	16
4 cups	cooked long grain white rice, cooled	1 L
⅓ lb	small cooked salad shrimp, fresh or frozen (and thawed), patted dry	170 g
1	14 oz (398 mL) can cut young (baby) corn	1
2 Tbsp	soy sauce	30 mL
to taste	freshly ground black pepper	to taste
3	green onions, thinly sliced	3

Heat the oil in a wok or very large skillet over medium-high heat. Add the pork and cook 3 to 4 minutes, or until cooked through. Mix in the onion and bell pepper and cook 1 minute more. Add the snow peas and cook 30 seconds more. Mix in the remaining ingredients and stir-fry 3 to 4 minutes, or until all the ingredients are well heated through. Serve immediately.

SAFFRON PARSLEY
MASHED POTATOES

preparation time · 10 minutes
cooking time · 20 minutes
makes · 6–8 servings

The crumbled threads of saffron give these mashed potatoes a golden hue and a very subtle, bitter honey–like taste. Saffron threads are sold in small bottles at most supermarkets and fine food stores. The best quality saffron has discernable threads and is a vivid, orangey red color.

ERIC'S OPTIONS
If you like onion, replace the parsley with 2 to 3 green onions, thinly sliced. Add after beating in the butter and milk.

3 lb	russet or baking potatoes, peeled and quartered	1.5 kg
1 tsp	crumbled saffron threads	5 mL
¼ cup	melted butter	60 mL
¾ cup	warm milk	175 mL
to taste	salt and white pepper	to taste
2 Tbsp	chopped fresh parsley	30 mL

Place the potatoes and saffron in a pot and cover with at least 2 inches (5 cm) of cold water. Bring the potatoes to a gentle boil (the water should just gently bubble) and cook until they are very tender but still hold their shape, about 20 minutes, depending on size. Drain well and thoroughly mash. Vigorously beat in the butter and milk until well combined and the potatoes are lightened. Season with salt and pepper; mix in the parsley and serve.

COLORFUL
VEGETABLE MEDLEY

preparation time · 15 minutes
cooking time · 12 minutes
makes · 8 servings

Red, green, orange and white vegetables make a colorful side dish to serve with roasts, fish, steaks and other entrées. The vegetables can be readied up to a day in advance and heated when needed.

ERIC'S OPTIONS
Give this dish an Italian-style flair by omitting the parsley and tossing in 2 to 3 Tbsp (30 to 45 mL) of pesto when heating the vegetables through. Sprinkle with freshly grated Parmesan cheese just before serving.

1 lb	baby carrots	500 g
32	cauliflower florets, each about 1 inch (2.5 cm) across	32
½ lb	snap peas, tops trimmed	250 g
1	large red bell pepper, cut into small cubes	1
2 Tbsp	butter	30 mL
1 cup	chicken or vegetable stock	250 mL
1	garlic clove, crushed	1
to taste	salt and freshly ground black pepper	to taste
1 Tbsp	chopped fresh parsley	15 mL

Place the carrots in a pot and cover with a generous amount of cold water. Boil until just tender but still a little firm. Add the cauliflower, snap peas and bell pepper, return to a boil, and cook 2 to 3 minutes more. Drain well, cool the vegetables in ice-cold water, and drain well again. (They can be prepared to this point a day in advance. Cover and refrigerate until needed.)

Place the butter, stock and garlic in a very large skillet and bring to a simmer; add the vegetables and heat through. Season with salt and pepper. Sprinkle the parsley overtop and serve.

MANDARIN CRANBERRY TARTS with GANACHE

preparation time	·	30 minutes plus chilling time
cooking time	·	15 minutes
makes	·	12 tarts

Take ganache, a dreamy mixture of melted chocolate and whipping cream, add sweet segments of fresh mandarin orange and tangy cranberries, and you have a dessert that's irresistible and also beautiful to present.

ERIC'S OPTIONS
The tarts can be filled with the ganache and refrigerated up to a day in advance of serving. Top with the oranges, cranberries, icing sugar and mint, if using, just before serving. For a more exotic-looking tart, substitute small slices of fresh fig for half the mandarin orange segments. In summer, omit the oranges and cranberries and top the tarts with summer berries, such as blackberries, blueberries and raspberries.

NOTE
Frozen, ready-to-use tart shells are sold at most supermarkets.

12	frozen 3-inch (8 cm) tart shells (see Note)	12
⅓ cup	whipping cream	75 mL
4 oz	semisweet chocolate, chopped	125 g
1 Tbsp	orange liqueur	15 mL
4	mandarin oranges, peeled and separated into segments	4
¼ cup	dried cranberries	60 mL
for dusting	icing sugar	for dusting
12	small mint sprigs, for garnish (optional)	12

Preheat the oven to 350°F (180°C). Place the tart shells on a baking sheet and prick each one several times with a fork. Bake until golden brown, about 15 minutes. Cool to room temperature. Remove the foil liners and set the tart shells on a serving tray.

Place the whipping cream in a small pot and bring to a boil. Add the chocolate and orange liqueur and stir until the chocolate is melted and well incorporated. Spoon the ganache into the tart shells, cool to room temperature and then refrigerate until the ganache is set, about 1 hour.

Decorate the tarts with orange segments and dried cranberries. To serve, dust the tarts lightly with icing sugar. Garnish with a mint sprig, if desired.

ROASTED PEARS with RUM and SPICE

preparation time · 20 minutes
cooking time · 30–35 minutes
makes · 6 servings

The deluxe look and taste of this pear dessert belies how simple it is to make. Buy the best-quality vanilla ice cream you can find.

ERIC'S OPTIONS
If you don't want to use alcohol, replace the rum with unsweetened apple juice.

6	generous scoops vanilla ice cream	6
3 Tbsp	butter, softened	45 mL
3 Tbsp	fresh lemon juice	45 mL
3	medium, slightly underripe pears	3
½ cup	maple syrup	125 mL
¼ cup	rum	60 mL
½ tsp	ground cinnamon	2 mL
pinch	ground nutmeg and cloves	pinch
6	fresh mint sprigs (optional)	6

Place a scoop of ice cream in each of 6 decorative bowls or glasses. Place in the freezer until needed. Preheat the oven to 350°F (180°C). Brush the bottom of a 9- × 13-inch (3.5 L) baking dish with the butter and set aside.

Place the lemon juice in a medium bowl. Peel the pears and quarter each lengthwise. Remove the cores from the pears. Add the pear quarters to the bowl and toss to coat with the lemon juice. Place the pears, core side up, in the baking dish. Combine the maple syrup, rum, cinnamon, nutmeg and cloves in a small bowl. Pour the mixture over the pears. Roast the pears, uncovered, for 15 minutes. Remove from the oven and use a small spoon to baste the top of the pears with the maple syrup mixture. Roast the pears 15 to 20 minutes, or until tender and nicely glazed.

Place 2 pear quarters in each serving of ice cream. Drizzle with the syrupy mixture in the baking dish. Garnish each dessert with a mint sprig, if desired, and serve.

HOW TO SERVE SPARKLING WINE

Champagne and other sparkling wines are the perfect, bubbly drink to pour for a celebration such as New Year's Eve. Here's how to serve it.

The chill
Sparkling wine should be served cold, at around 45°F (7°C). If it's too cold, the flavor and aroma of the wine can be stunted. If it's too warm, the wine can foam too much and lose its bubbles when poured. The ideal temperature can be achieved in two ways. The wine can be refrigerated for 3 to 4 hours, or, if you're in a hurry, you can place the unopened bottle in an ice bucket filled with an equal mixture of ice and water for about 20 minutes. When it's at the correct temperature, it should feel very cold, not just cool, when you put your hand on the bottle.

The glass
Sparkling wine is best served in tall, slender flutes or glasses that show the wine bubbles to best advantage as they ascend from the bottom of the glass to the top. The glasses must be sparkling clean; if they're not, the wine can lose its bubble.

The uncorking
When removing the foil and wire hood from the top of the bottle, secure the cork with your thumb or finger, preventing it from prematurely slipping out. Hold the bottle at a 45-degree angle away from you and anyone else. While firmly holding the cork, gently turn the bottom of the bottle—not the cork. The cork should ease out of the bottle with a gentle pop, not release quickly with an explosive sound.

The pour
Clean the top and neck of the bottle with a cloth napkin. Pour 1 inch (2.5 cm) of wine into each glass. When the foam has settled, fill each glass two-thirds full. This technique prevents the wine from foaming too much and spilling out of the glass.

MENUS

I call this a "retro" menu, albeit an updated one, because it features names or styles of dishes that decades ago were staple items served in many fine-dining establishments. The appetizer course offers a choice of two such items: shrimp cocktail and raw oysters.

Ever-popular onion soup, traditionally topped with a crouton and melted Swiss cheese, is updated with a decadent crumbled Stilton cheese instead.

"Surf and turf" was on every menu in the 1970s and it's on this one, too, pairing a tender steak with succulent crab-stuffed mushrooms. Serve the steaks with baked potatoes and a simple green vegetable, such as green beans.

Warm fruit desserts flavored with butter, sugar and booze, such as bananas flambé, were popular way back when—this menu for 6 reestablishes that trend with the roasted pears with rum.

- Shrimp Cocktail Canapés (page 231) or Oysters on the Half Shell with Dill Red Pepper Vinaigrette (page 232)
- Onion Soup with Crumbled Stilton (page 229)
- Beef Tenderloin Steaks with Crab-Stuffed Mushrooms (page 238)
- Roasted Pears with Rum and Spice (page 248)

ELEGANT NEW YEAR'S DAY DINNER

This menu for 6 marks the new year with a fine array of dishes that are remarkably easy to prepare. Most of these dishes can also be prepared partially or entirely in advance. After the soup, you could serve a simple green salad to cleanse your palate before the main course.

- New Year's Day Punch (page 221)
- Parsnip and Pear Soup with Balsamic-Maple Drizzle (page 227)
- Roast Strip Loin with Dijon and Herbes de Provence (page 240)
- No-Fuss Yorkshire Puddings (page 241)

- Saffron Parsley Mashed Potatoes (page 244)
- Colorful Vegetable Medley (page 245)
- Mandarin Cranberry Tarts with Ganache (page 246)

DON'T-RISE-TOO-EARLY NEW YEAR'S DAY BREAKFAST

Stay up late ringing in the New Year, sleep in the next morning and then wake up in style with this breakfast featuring a sparkling drink, fluffy pancakes, healthy, delicious breakfast meat and a colorful mix of fresh fruit soaked in a ginger-laced syrup.

- Sparkling Lemon Pomegranate Spritzers (page 220)
- Morning Glory Pancakes (page 225)
- Pork and Oat Sausage Patties (page 226)
- Mixed Fruit Cocktail in Ginger Syrup (page 222)

CHINESE NEW YEAR DINNER BUFFET

Chinese New Year, often called the Lunar New Year, is an important celebration in China and in areas with populations of ethnic Chinese, such as you'll find in cities across North America, including my home, Victoria, BC. Each year, many folks of Chinese origin and otherwise, head down to our city's Chinatown for special meals and events. You can also celebrate the "good luck" spirit of Chinese New Year by serving a Chinese-style dinner at home, such as this one. Accompany the meal with Chinese tea. At the end the meal, hand out fortune cookies, which you can buy at Chinese food markets and in the Asian food aisle of some supermarkets.

- Emerald and White Jade Soup (page 230)
- The Emperor's Fried Rice (page 242)
- Shrimp and Mixed Vegetable Chow Mein (page 235)
- Chinese-Style Barbecue Chicken (page 237)

INDEX

"Eric Akis is a fine chef who understands simplicity and finesse in cooking. His book is modern home cooking, with easy-to-make recipes that are honest, free-wheeling and mouth-watering. It is the perfect kitchen companion. Keep it by your stove and refer to it often!"
GARY HYNES, EDITOR, *EAT MAGAZINE*

"I will be reaching for *Everyone Can Cook* just as I reach for my favourite cooking pot. Now I can throw away my tattered collection of Eric's columns. It is user friendly and the results are delicious—the perfect combination."
NOEL RICHARDSON, BESTSELLING FOOD WRITER AND CO-OWNER OF RAVENHILL FARM

"Eric's creative and straightforward recipes make me want to invite friends over for seafood—tonight!"
RON EADE, FOOD EDITOR, *OTTAWA CITIZEN*

"This book is a celebration of our oceans' bounty, well researched and beautifully executed. Eric Akis is a home cook who knows how to write a recipe the way home cooks like. They are uncomplicated, easy to understand and make the main ingredient (seafood) the star. Bravo Eric!"
KARL WELLS, FOOD CHAIN, CBC COUNTRY CANADA CHANNEL

"It's odd that a definitive Canadian seafood book has not been written before now, given that the country has the longest coastline of earth. Well, the wait is over . . . this is IT!"
ANITA STEWART, AUTHOR AND CULINARY ACTIVIST

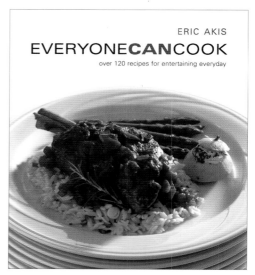

ISBN 978-1-55285-448-8

ISBN 978-1-55285-614-7

"No cookbooks in my collection are more dogeared than *Everyone Can Cook* and *Everyone Can Cook Seafood*. Thank you, Eric, for dishing up this brilliant new volume of appetizers and tantalizing our taste buds once again!"
ELIZABETH LEVINSON, AWARD-WINNING AUTHOR AND COLUMNIST FOR *FOCUS* MAGAZINE

"The real joy of food is sharing. In his latest book, Eric continues his tradition of sharing creative, elegant and real food recipes. I predict many happy parties and family gatherings will be fuelled by this delicious book."
BILL JONES, CHEF, AUTHOR AND FOOD CONSULTANT

"Do you know what's in that meatball? With Eric Akis's help you will, and your family will be healthier for it. Even the most time-challenged and inexperienced cook will find much inspiration here."
RENEE BLACKSTONE, FOOD AND WINE EDITOR OF THE *PROVINCE* (VANCOUVER)

"Eric Akis is my kind of Superman. In his latest recipe collection, he offers more than what we have come to expect of him—food clearly explained. He serves it all forth with genuine goodwill and wry humor, the telltale sign of a true Clark Kent beneath the cape. With this culinary crusader's gentle guidance, we can all cook."
DEE HOBSBAWN-SMITH, CHEF, EDUCATOR AND AUTHOR OF *THE CURIOUS COOK AT HOME*

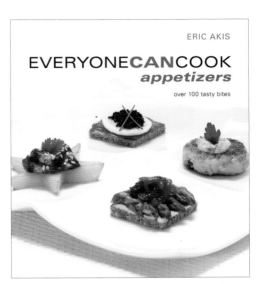

ISBN 978-1-55285-793-9

ISBN 978-1-55285-924-7

ABOUT THE AUTHOR

Eric Akis has been food writer for the *Victoria Times Colonist* since 1997. His columns are published in newspapers across Canada.

Prior to becoming a journalist, Akis trained to become a professional chef and pastry chef. He worked for 15 years in a variety of operations in Ontario and British Columbia, from fine hotels to restaurants to catering companies.

In 2003, his experiences as a chef and food writer inspired him to create the bestselling Everyone Can Cook series of cookbooks, which includes *Everyone Can Cook, Everyone Can Cook Seafood, Everyone Can Cook Appetizers, Everyone Can Cook Midweek Meals* and now *Everyone Can Cook for Celebrations.*

Eric Akis was born into a military family in Chicoutimi, Quebec, and has lived in six provinces. Victoria, BC, where he moved in 1992, is now officially home, where he lives with his wife, Cheryl Warwick, also a chef, and son, Tyler.